the Jesus Connection

the
Jesus
Connection

A
Christian
Spirituality

Jan G. Linn

CHALICE™
P R E S S

ST. LOUIS, MISSOURI

Biblical quotations, unless otherwise noted, are from the *New Revised Standard Version Bible*, copyright 1989, Division of Christian Education of the National Council of the Churches of Christ in the USA. Used by permission.

Cover Design: Lynne Condellone and Howard Schröder

Visit Chalice Press on the World Wide Web at
www.chalicepress.com

10 9 8 7 6 5 4 3   04 05

Library of Congress Cataloging-in-Publication Data

Linn, Jan.
   The Jesus connection: a Christian spirituality / Jan G. Linn
         p.   cm.
   Includes bibliographical references
   ISBN 0-8272-1709-9
   1. Spirituality--Christianity. 2. Jesus Christ--Person and offices. I. Title.
   BV4509.5.L56   1997
   248--dc21
                                        96-6503
                                            CIP

Printed in the United States of America

FOR JOY

ACKNOWLEDGMENTS

This book has emerged from the numerous and varied influences that have helped to form me as a person of faith. It is, therefore, impossible to identify all the people to whom I owe so much in so many different ways. I am thinking of family members, Sunday School teachers, parents of childhood friends, and many others whose faith and commitment to the church made such an impression on me at an early age. I am thinking of the lasting impression a high-profile professional athlete made on me so many years ago now when he came to my high school to speak and gave an unexpected, and not altogether positively received, testimony about what Jesus Christ meant to his life. I am thinking of seminary teachers whose ability to balance faith and scholarship was a source of encouragement, and theological mentors whose lives were models of what I wanted to be. These are the hidden influences that have made the writing of this book possible.

Others—colleagues and friends—have made a more direct contribution to this work, and those I want to name: Sharyn Dowd, Rick Landon, and Charles Bayer, who read portions of it; special thanks to

Bill McGraw, Larry Paul Jones, Malcom Warford, and Bonnie Jones, all of whom read the entire manuscript. While the weaknesses of the book are solely mine, I want to thank each of these colleagues publicly for making this a better book than it would have been without their suggestions and comments.

To the many students in my spiritual formation classes I want to express sincere gratitude for their openness to the concepts and ideas found in the book, and for their comments through the years which have contributed to clarity and refinement of the material. Appreciation also goes to the participants in several church gatherings who asked challenging questions that helped sharpen my own thinking as I worked on this material. They include: South Park Christian Church, Charlotte, North Carolina, and pastor and friend Jerry Whitt; Park Hill Christian Church, Kansas City, and pastors Larry Patterson and Richard Weaver; and the Ministers and Mates of the Christian Church in Tennessee and Regional Minister Glen Stewart.

I especially want to express my continuing gratitude to the staff at Chalice Press for the opportunity to work with them. Special thanks to David Polk for his encouragement to put in writing the ideas that shape my own life and ministry. Editors are a special breed, the behind-the-scenes folk whose patience, persistence, and critical eye not only make books possible, but make them better than they otherwise would be. They seldom get the credit they deserve.

Finally, I want to express love and gratitude for my wife, Joy. Her own experience in ministry gives her the ability to read what I write with an eye for what is real. More than that, she possesses an enviable self-confidence that frees her to love me enough to tell me the truth, but to do it with gentleness and unwavering support. She is my best friend. She is a gift. Thus, the book's dedication to her.

CONTENTS

INTRODUCTION

I sat listening as the speaker called on the church to take spirituality seriously. He spoke with sincerity and passion about this need. He went so far as to say that without a spiritual foundation the church has no power or direction. After a few minutes he moved to a second point he was making about the challenges facing mainline Protestant churches in North America today. My mind did not go with him. My thoughts lingered on his first point. There was nothing that he said about spirituality that initially was troubling. Actually, it was refreshing to hear a church leader address the subject. Yet something seemed to be lacking. Finally it dawned on me that the speaker had never defined spirituality, and certainly not in terms that were particularly Christian. While his remarks were religious, that is, they made explicit reference to God, they could just as easily have been made to a non-Christian gathering.

In an age of religious pluralism, it is common to hear Christians talk about a kind of generic spirituality. Hardly any overt or direct connection is made between spirituality and the Christian gospel. Whether this is conscious or not is unclear, but that it is commonplace seems evident. At best Jesus is cited as an example of someone who prayed and knew his tradition. Omission of anything that has to do with Jesus as Savior and Lord or the central role he must play in the Christian's life may account in part for the perception among many church members that mainline church leaders cannot speak with conviction about what it means to be Christian in today's world.

It seems we have arrived at the point where many mainline church leaders resist anything that smacks of Christian particularism. The situation seems to me to be neither theologically defensible nor personally satisfying. While the realities of religious pluralism have changed the landscape of American society, it does not require a retreat among Christians in witnessing to Jesus Christ. The fact that some Christians use theological dogma with which to beat all non-Christians, and not a few Christians, over the head does not mean the majority of mainline Christians are unable or unwilling to recognize and embrace the potential benefit of such religious diversity. What they do not understand, and rightfully so, is why the particularity of Christian faith by definition disregards respect for other religious traditions. Nor do they believe that inclusivity requires the church to reject limits to theological diversity within its own household. The notion prevalent among many mainline theologians and clergy that there is a non-negotiable "center" for Christian faith strikes them as an example of extreme relativism they cannot and will not accept as a rule of faith. Rather, they believe the New Testament and the best of the Christian tradition through the centuries are unequivocal in claiming that Jesus Christ is that center and do not understand why that is so difficult for church leaders to affirm. It is not surprising that many laity have a sense that their leaders can no longer speak with confidence or clarity about the meaning of Jesus for salvation.

I do not believe the best leaders in the church today have reached the point of outright rejection of the centrality of Jesus Christ to the Christian community's life and witness. But I do believe the church is experiencing what rightly can be called theological "slippage," meaning a movement away from articulating faith for Christians within Christ-centered boundaries. The undefined, ill-defined, and bland discussion of spirituality commonplace among church leaders today reflects this "slippage." This book is my attempt to address this problem. It begins with the conviction that *spirituality in the church ought to have something tangible to say about its relationship to Jesus Christ.* In other words, I contend that Christian spirituality is inextricably bound to the claims of the New Testament in its proclamation of the life, death and resurrection of Jesus Christ as Savior and Lord.

Can this be done without joining the ranks of self-righteous Christians who are not content with being the people of God, but who must be the only people of God? I believe it can. The validity of the Christian gospel does not depend upon the invalidity of all other religious traditions. It stands on its own merit. It is self-authenticating precisely because that is the mystical nature of Christian faith. A basic conviction guiding this work is that the greater the intimacy Christians have with the One who is the heart of the gospel, the more open-minded and openhearted they become toward non-Christians.

From this basic argument I seek to describe the experience of Christian spirituality in detail, noting signs of spiritual growth, discussing the role of the Holy Spirit, addressing the importance of personal discipline, identifying various ways of praying, speaking to the common experience of discouragement when we seek to take Christian spirituality seriously, and concluding with a discussion of some signs of spiritually mature congregations.

I believe it is possible that the present may be a "kairos" time in the life of the church here in the United States. The hunger among people, Christian and non-Christian, even religious and nonreligious, for something—anything—that can help them connect with God or the transcendent is an urgent invitation to churches and church leaders to speak boldly, albeit humbly, about the particular faith that gives us life and hope. Moreover, Christians and churches that desire to be renewed themselves must begin to practice spirituality in a serious way. And that means recovering the heart of the Christian gospel, which is the essential connectedness Christians have with Jesus. I do not believe either personal or collective renewal will occur without our attending to this divine/human connection.

For this reason I suggest that time be spent working with the material in each chapter before moving to the next. In classes that I teach in spirituality, I challenge the members to ask themselves what is helpful in the books they read, rather than reading the material only to note what they agree or disagree with. This assignment is a way of getting them to test ideas with their own experience as well as belief. When they make the effort to read in this way, more often than not the books make a lasting impact on them. I share this teaching method as a way to invite readers to put this book to such a test. Perhaps it might then make a contribution to genuine renewal.

1

SPIRITUALITY
AND JESUS

*Christian spirituality
is founded on Jesus.*

Jean Vanier

Spirituality is a popular subject in many religious
and quasi-religious circles today, including churches of all stripes, para-
church groups, groups in other religious traditions, and numerous self-
help groups that make no explicit religious claims. This widespread
interest in spirituality has even caught the attention of news organizations. A local television station in my city recently had a report on the
feature section of its evening news on the subject of prayer. The pop
psychology folks who write best-selling books that tell us how to have
better love relationships now hold workshops on such topics as "The
Spirituality of Sex" and "The Spirituality of Making Up."

In the church, conversations about the need for spiritual renewal
abound at various levels. Spirituality has replaced techniques of effective management as a popular subject of workshops seeking to attract
church leaders. In 1995 the Alban Institute, a church consulting group
whose self-defining mission is "to gather, generate, and provide practical knowledge across denominational lines," held workshops across the
country on such topics as "Nourishing Spirituality in Congregations,"
"Pastor as Spiritual Leader," and "Spirituality of Aging." Its recent publications on spirituality include books on spiritual growth through small

groups and a guide to identifying individual and congregational "spiritual types." Perusing the church section of local newspapers in most cities of any size, one will find numerous invitations to lectures and workshops on spirituality.

It is worth noting that the current interest in spirituality within the church, however contemporary its cast may be, has deep roots in the Christian tradition. Marjorie Thompson points out that the common usage of the word *spirituality* is a replacement of traditional words once very familiar in the church, such as *piety* and *devotion* (Thompson, 5).† The point is that we should not lose sight of the fact that the focus today on spirituality in the church is not a new phenomenon. It only seems so, probably because the subject has caught on in the larger society.

This popular interest in spirituality can be seen by Christians as an encouraging development, a sign that society has come to a dead end with its preoccupation with self and materialism and is searching for something deeper. As such, the situation invites the church to point people to a different way. But I suggest that the church also needs to be asking some basic questions about spirituality before things go too far, if they have not already. It is a good rule of thumb to think through one's response to a genuine need before offering help, lest the help given make matters worse rather than better. Such caution may sound a bit strange, but I hope to show that it is not strange at all, that in fact there is good evidence that the "pop" spirituality we are seeing so much of today offers far less than what people really need. Moreover, the church has not recognized, for various reasons, the inoculation dangers inherent in the situation. That is, what passes for spirituality in many instances is little more than a vaccination that gives one a little bit of the disease without getting the whole thing.

I believe this is precisely the effect of generic spirituality within the context of the Christian community. That is, generic spirituality in the church gets baptized without being able to offer the full measure of meaning and power that life in Jesus Christ gives. The material in the

---

†See the Selected Bibliography at the end of this book for fuller references to works cited.

following pages arose from my belief in and experience with the gospel that convinced me that it offers something more, something much deeper, something with greater substance, than a "higher power" kind of spirituality because it is rooted in who Jesus Christ was and is, and our relationship with him today. The only way to understand and to experience this kind of spirituality is to consider its relationship to Jesus. Other than being a cause for rejoicing, examples of non-Christian spiritual giants such as Gandhi and the Dalai Lama matter little in the church. What does matter is for Christians to find their way spiritually within their own faith tradition. I am of the mind that help in this regard in churches today is anemic at best, and absent altogether in many instances.

The basic question to ask, if we are to move away from generic spirituality in the church, is "What is 'Christian' about spirituality?" Is there such a thing as "Christian" spirituality, and if so, what is it? What is distinctive about it? While acknowledging that Christians do not hold a corner on spirituality, is there any basis for believing that for Christians spirituality can be "Christian" in content and in practice? Does it have anything to do with the claim that Jesus is both Savior and Lord of the church? Or must we finally admit that while Jesus may have been an example of a spiritual leader, the rest of the story, that is, his crucifixion and resurrection are quaint stories about the refusal of his first disciples to give up a good idea? I want to argue that Christian spirituality offers more than an idea or an example in Jesus. It is an invitation to know him, experience him, love him, and belong to him.

There are, however, reasons for caution we would be wise to note as we begin this journey. For one thing, it is important for Christians to realize that Christian spirituality involves faith and experience. That is, it has to do with belief and personal encounter. These are not in tension with each other but exist to strengthen both. Genuine Christian spirituality concerns the informing and transforming of both the mind and the heart, as we shall discuss later. For now it is important to note that any separation of theology and experience, belief and action, is a false dichotomy.

Second, the church will have to be intentional in reaffirming and refocusing some of its thinking and energy on the personal nature of faith. In the last thirty years or so, mainline churches have appropriately devoted attention to many worthwhile concerns that have to do with living the faith we say we have, with what might be called the "works" of faith. This emphasis on action certainly should not be abandoned. Genuine spirituality includes both contemplation and action, to use the words of Thomas Merton.

But I believe it is fair to say that, commensurate with an emphasis on deeds, has been too little intentional attention to the life of the Spirit, too much emphasis on the "fruits" of faith while neglecting the "roots." Our mission has been one of getting church members into the world doing the gospel on behalf of others, encouraging them into Christian action and service. But we have done so without sufficient spiritual nurture.

The Church of The Savior in Washington, D.C., is a faith community known for its social ministries. But what is not always understood is the fact that for them ministry is deeply rooted in prayer. Elizabeth O'Connor has sought to make this clear in the books she has written about the church. A theme she repeats is that the problem is not that the church is not in the world, as many church critics say. The real problem, she says, is that the church is in the world without being sent. By this she means the church's sense of mission does not arise from its spiritual life.

Yet this is what has happened in mainline churches across the board. The call to mission has not been accompanied by a call to prayer, to attending to the spiritual life of church members. As a consequence, they have been left pretty much to fend for themselves regarding their spiritual needs. The result has been that many of them have gone outside the church for help.

A renewal, if not recovery, of Christian spirituality in the church today depends upon this refocused attention to the personal nature of faith. But for this to happen, church leaders will have to rethink a long-entrenched suspicion of personal religious experience. Quite telling was a 1990 survey among Episcopalians in which 42 percent of the respondents reported having had a "life-changing religious experience," while Episcopal leaders, especially at judicatory levels, dismissed such experiences as examples of untutored "emotionalism" (Reed, 13).

While this data is particular to Episcopalians, it reflects the dominance of enlightenment liberalism within mainline Protestant churches (and to some extent the Roman Catholic Church as well) that gave rise to a suspicion of anything not steeped in rationalism. This suspicion regarding personal religious experience may account for safe talk about spirituality in mainline churches, such as the spirituality of stewardship, of leadership, of small groups; or talking about spirituality only in terms of a God who is gracious and loving, or about following the example Jesus set. All of these may be helpful, but none addresses the basic issue of a Christian spirituality that is centered in a personal relationship with the raised Jesus.

A third caution is the need to be conscious of the potential for spiritual elitism, the epitome of an unchristian attitude. It would be easy for the kind of discussion we are engaged in to degenerate into divisive judgmentalism similar to what the Apostle Paul encountered in Corinth regarding the gift of speaking in tongues. My concern throughout is not who is more spiritual than another, or who is or is not practicing a truly Christian spirituality. Rather, the real intention is to describe an understanding and practice of spirituality that is rooted in the Christian gospel for mainline church members who struggle with either faith or experience when it comes to Jesus. I believe our churches are full of people who want to make connection with Jesus in a personal way but do not know how. They can talk about God, but Jesus is a different matter. Even using the name Jesus without the title "Christ" or "the Christ" is something with which they are not altogether very comfortable. They may know something about the teachings of Jesus but little about belonging to him. They may believe in the death and resurrection of Jesus, but the event remains a biblical account of the past.

This is not to deny the fact that there are Christian sects and individuals who are guilty of what is sometimes described as "a unitarianism of the second Person of the Trinity," that is, a focus on Jesus to the exclusion of either God or the Holy Spirit. Nonetheless, I believe most Christians of various stripes have a genuine desire to be in a vital and personal relationship to Jesus Christ. They have a desire for a much deeper experience of faith than they have. They are beyond mere interest in spirituality. They are hungry for it.

It is for these Christians that this material has been written. It is for Christians who need help in developing a relationship with Jesus that is real but does not require them to park their brains or their humanitarian concerns outside the church door. It is for Christians who have no interest in proving the supremacy of Christianity and the invalidity of all other religions, but who do have a profound need to know the reality of the resurrection they already believe in but have never experienced. It is written for Christians who struggle with how to live faithfully and honestly as people who claim the name of Jesus for their lives. It is written for Christians who want more than they are getting, who want to give more than they are giving, but who want and need some help.

So we come back to the question asked earlier: "What is spirituality for Christians, and what makes it particularly Christian?" The question has two related yet distinct parts. The first has to do with the *ends* of Christian spirituality, the other has to do with the *means*. The two are often confused by Christian teachers, preachers, and writers, which accounts for the lack of clarity about what makes spirituality Christian. My thesis is that the means of Christian spirituality, which is Jesus Christ, is what sets Christian spirituality apart. We shall discuss this in detail in a moment. But first we need to describe the ends of Christian spirituality, that is, what it is. As we begin, let me invite the reader to bracket "how to" about spirituality at this point. The practice of Christian spirituality will be addressed at the end of this chapter and in more detail in later ones. For the moment, however, we need to attend to its meaning, its Christological foundations, if you will.

A guide to our thinking on the ends and means of a Christian spirituality is John 21:15-17, which is the post-resurrection story of Jesus meeting the disciples at the Galilean seashore. During this encounter with the raised Jesus, Peter is confronted three times with the same question: "Do you love me?" After each answer Peter gives, Jesus directs him to perform a task ("Feed my lambs….Tend my sheep….Feed my sheep").

This passage offers a mirror into which we look to see ourselves. In doing so, we hear Jesus speaking to us as well as to Peter. His question to Peter, "Do you love me?" challenges us to confront the nature of our relationship to him. In terms of Christian spirituality, his question has to do with means. That is, how do we become spiritually mature Christians? But before we get into the means, we first must deal with the ends toward which Christian spirituality points us. This end has to do with the tasks Jesus set before Peter—and us—in this passage. What Jesus tells Peter each time is to do ministry. He commissions him to service. And the heart of this ministry is this: *To Love the Way Jesus Loved!* This is what Jesus wanted Peter to go out and do. This is the "ends" of Christian spirituality, the goal toward which we as Christians are to journey. We are to love the way Jesus loved in all our relationships. Jesus' own life becomes the paradigm for the way we are to live as his disciples in today's world.

This, of course, is no simple or easy task. Indeed, it can appropriately and rightly be described as "cross spirituality." For loving this way is a bold and radical act that often requires pain and sacrifice. It begins with the cross of Jesus and leads to the cross we must also bear. Jesus said that to follow him, i.e., love him, we must pick up our cross. The cross stands before anyone who chooses to give allegiance to Jesus. This cross is to love the way he loved no matter what!

Generally Christians think of bearing some personal burden or making some personal sacrifice as the cross we must carry as followers of Jesus. Burden and sacrifice are, as we said, a part of serious discipleship. But they are not in themselves the cross we are to bear. Rather, the cross we must bear is the cross of loving the way Jesus loved. Herein is the most profoundly difficult thing Christians must do. Nothing offers a greater challenge or demands of us a more exacting sacrifice than to love the way Jesus loved. There is nothing easy about it. It takes all we are to do it, and then some. But it is what we must do because it is, as we shall see, who we are as disciples of Jesus.

Loving the way Jesus loved is a call to action. It challenges Christians to a life of loving justice-seeking. This is why Paul said that a summary of the law could be found in the words, "Love your neighbor as yourself" (Romans 13:9). Then he added, "Love does no wrong to a neighbor; therefore, love is the fulfilling of the law." (Romans 13:10.)

This text suggests what I believe the entire New Testament says, that loving the way Jesus loved is the cross we must bear as his disciples. This is the primary mark of Christian obedience. What is more, Jesus himself said this kind of love for one another would be the distinguishing mark by which the world would know that we are his disciples (John 13:35). But let's explore the kind of love Jesus modeled. The New Testament as a whole, and the Gospels in particular, remember Jesus as loving without the artificial and often unjust walls and barriers that usually separate people. A startling and poignant illustration of this is the encounter Jesus had with a Canaanite woman (Matthew 15:21–28; Mark 7:24–30). She comes to Jesus to ask him to heal her daughter. The disciples urge him to send the woman away because she is not Jewish. Jesus' initial response reflects this kind of artificial barrier. But the woman persists, pleading for Jesus to have compassion for her daughter. The daughter is healed. The story's candor is arresting. The woman's faith in Jesus' healing power becomes the key factor in Jesus' recognizing and ultimately rejecting the barrier between Jews and non-Jews that the disciples want him to observe.

The Gospels tell us of other instances where Jesus modeled loving beyond artificial barriers separating people. He talked to a Samaritan woman (John 4:1–27), healed a centurion's servant (Matthew 8:5–13), actually touched a leper (Matthew 8:1–3), and based upon criticisms of him, apparently shared meals with tax-collectors and other people believed to be sinners (Matthew 9:10–11). He identified his presence with the marginalized—the poor, the sick, the imprisoned, the victims of injustice (Matthew 25:31–46). He loved without allowing premature judgments to influence his attitude toward another (Luke 19:1–10), loving people enough to call forth the best within them, standing with them, crying out with them.

This is the kind of love that wants to be a good neighbor, that wants to build bridges rather than barriers. The story of Ruby Bridges is a winsome example of what this kind of love looks like in today's world. Psychiatrist Robert Coles of Harvard Medical School and winner of the Pulitzer Prize for his multivolume work, *Children of Crisis*, has spent a lifetime telling Ruby's story. His experience with Ruby in 1960 permanently changed his life. Ruby was a six-year-old African American first-grader who was assigned to attend Franz School, an all-white public school, as part of a federal court order related to the desegregation of the public school system in New Orleans. Every morning and afternoon she was escorted by federal marshals through an angry crowd of two hundred white demonstrators threatening to kill her. Ruby was the only child in the school each day because of the all-white boycott. Coles, a child psychiatrist who had studied the psychological trauma serious physical illness had on children, wanted to study the effects this emotional trauma was having on Ruby. Through a long and complicated process he gained permission to talk with her. In a film about his life and career, Coles describes what happened in his conversations with Ruby (see Baird-Middleton).

At first she had very little to say about what was going on or how she felt about it. They spent a lot of their time together making crayon and watercolor drawings. One day her teacher told Coles that she saw Ruby stop, say something to the crowd, and then continue her walk through this jeering mob into the school. That night at Ruby's home, while they were drawing pictures, Coles asked her to whom she was talking when she walked through the crowd that morning. She replied she was not talking to anyone. Concerned that if she didn't express the anger and fear she must be feeling, Ruby could quickly get into trouble emotionally—that she could become seriously depressed—Coles said he began to push. He told Ruby the teacher had seen her stop and saw her lips moving as she looked at the crowd, so she must have been talking to someone. Ruby replied that she wasn't talking to the people. She was talking to God. Coles was intrigued. He asked Ruby what she said to God. She answered that she didn't say anything, that she was praying to God. He was really intrigued by this, he said, sure that further exploration would begin to reveal the trauma he knew she had to be experiencing. He asked Ruby what it was she prayed. She replied that she prayed the same thing each morning and each afternoon. Coles asked her what that was. Ruby replied, "I pray that God will forgive them because they don't know what they're doing."

Ruby's response silenced Coles. Here was this little six-year-old child who was going through a horrible experience, and she was praying for the people who were threatening to kill her. Deeply moved by what Ruby said and by who she was, Coles went on to make a critical decision in his professional life that he attributes to his encounter with Ruby.

He chose to move away from traditional psychoanalytic child psychiatry to a focus on what he now calls documentary psychiatry, where he learned to talk with children going through their everyday lives amid substantial social and educational stress. More than this, though, his personal life was also dramatically affected. The witness of faith of little Ruby Bridges stirred Coles's soul, and he would later move from agnosticism to become a person of faith. All Ruby did was to practice with the innocence of a child the kind of neighborly love Jesus practiced. Such a small thing on the surface, yet her loving those who were threatening to kill her changed Robert Coles's life.

Of course there are circumstances in which how to witness to neighborly love is not easily discernable. This is because life is ambiguous. Reality will not be reduced to oversimplifications. Loving the way Jesus loved is not permissiveness rooted in an extreme relativism that cannot say No to anything. Nor is it incompatible with tough love. What is more, the call to neighborly love should not be used as an excuse for attempting to legislate morality for causes of either the left or right. Yet it is and always has been the kind of love that has the power to heal personal and social wounds, that has the staying power to work at transforming systemic causes of injustice. It is the kind of love that loves people enough to tell them the truth and calls them to greater faithfulness. It is the kind of love that works hard at balancing high standards with forgiveness, balancing expectations with understanding, balancing obedience with grace. It is the love for enemies of a little six-year-old girl that changed a grown man's life.

This kind of love has no limits to its dominion. It looks at the whole world as the dwelling place of God; it sees all forms of life as expressions of the face of God. It views the environment as a sanctuary for the Spirit of God and, thus, to be treated with reverence and respect that are the foundation for responsible stewardship.

This is not an easy road to walk (Jesus described living this way as being sheep among wolves, Matthew 10:16). Indeed, loving this way forces Christians to swim against the dominant currents of societal life. It is choosing to view the world with different eyes, choosing to live by God's claim on our lives rather than by what we claim in our lives, choosing to reach toward those from whom others turn away, choosing to share life with those others exclude, choosing to live as tenants rather than owners in a delicate balance with the whole of life. We make these choices for one reason. We are committed in our own lifetime to loving the way Jesus loved.

+ + +

Now we turn to the means of Christian spirituality. Here is to be found the particularity of spirituality for Christians. Non-Christians advocate justice-seeking. Non-Christians try to love without barriers. Non-Christians call the world to a reverence and respect for the whole of creation—all of which makes the end of Christian spirituality as we have been describing it hardly unique. It is only when the end is connected to the means that Christians practice a particularly Christian spirituality. Here we turn to the question Jesus put to Peter in the John 21 passage. Jesus asked Peter, "Do you love me?" Not, Do you believe in me? Not, Do you believe I have set the example for you to follow? Not, Do you understand all about me? It was simply, Do you love me?

This question defines the means, indeed, the heart of Christian spirituality. It is this: *To love Jesus!* This is the foundation of Christian spirituality. Further, it challenges the church's traditional interpretation of "feeding the sheep" as the means of loving Jesus. Such an interpretation collapses the means into the ends which turns discipleship into works righteousness. To focus on loving Jesus as the means of Christian spirituality is to underscore the personal relationship dimension of discipleship. Being a Christian is not just loving the way Jesus loved. It is also loving Jesus, being with him, knowing him, moving beyond belief to experience, beyond propositions to a relationship of love. This personal relationship is the power that makes loving the way Jesus loved possible. Before we do anything, what Jesus wants from us is what he wanted from Peter—love. This is a relationship that is more than trying to follow the teachings of a good man who lived in the first century. It is a living relationship because this Jesus was raised from the dead and lives today.

For this reason the means of Christian spirituality can appropriately and rightly be described as "resurrection spirituality." While belief in

Jesus as Savior and Lord is important, it is in the transformative moment or moments when one encounters the raised Jesus that the spiritual journey for Christians truly begins. We might even say that it begins with conversion, metanoia, that point in life when we decide to "turn away" from other claims and turn to Jesus. This is a decisive, transformative moment, a resurrection moment, when the Christian is raised to new life, "born again," in the best sense of that metaphor. This begins the formative process of growing and maturing in loving Jesus. It leads to the experience of learning the deepest meaning of being his followers, committed to him, belonging to him, and concerned that we are identified with him.

For Christians, loving Jesus provides a focus for the spiritual life—devotion and loyalty to him—that goes a step beyond belief. According to Matthew's Gospel, Jesus said as much himself in the Sermon on the Mount when he said: "But strive first for the kingdom of God and his righteousness, and all these things will be given to you as well" (6:33). The Matthean textual context for this challenge is Jesus' discussion of the nature of security. He acknowledges that we need food and clothing and shelter, but he also says bluntly that concern about any of these needs has the potential of causing us to forget that genuine security is to be found in God and nowhere else. In a helpful discussion of this text, Vernard Eller comments:

> As long as "'all' the rest" is so ordered as "to come to you as 'well,' to come 'after,' to come out of and consequent upon the 'first,'" then it has been provided with the control that will make it good, keep it good, and use it for good. But there is nothing—not one thing—in that "all the rest" that is inherently good enough in itself so that it can stand in place of or alongside of the 'first' without corrupting its own value and meaning in the process...to set one's mind upon [God's] kingdom is to seek, above all, to let [God's] will be done in one's life. (Eller, 20-21)

The point Eller makes is that there are no first "things." There is only one first thing—God. God is to be our first loyalty, our first priority, our first concern. Nothing else can stand equal to loyalty to God.

Because of the extraordinary claim of Christian faith that Jesus was God incarnate, acknowledging God as the only "first thing" means to be loyal to Jesus with single-mindedness. This is the kind of loyalty Jesus wanted from Peter, a loyalty he lacked when it was first put to the test. This kind of loyalty is "first-loyalty" love. It is love that puts our relationship to Jesus first, before anything and anyone else, as expressed in Colossians 1:18: "He is the head of the body, the church; he is the beginning, the firstborn from the dead, so that he might come to have first place *in everything*" (emphasis added).

First-loyalty love is the way we demonstrate what we believe, that we know our life as a Christian depends on our relationship to Jesus. In John 15:1-5 Jesus uses the metaphor of the vine and the branch to illustrate the essentialness of this relationship: "I am the vine, you are the branches" (15:5). A branch is utterly dependent upon the vine for its life. The vine is the life-source for the branch. It sustains and feeds the branch. The branch has no life apart from the vine. The implications of this metaphor should be clear. The Christian's life is utterly dependent on being connected to Jesus as the branch's life is connected to the vine. There is no life if we are separated from Jesus. He promises us that we will bear much fruit as we are connected to him. We will achieve the ends. But the crucial point is the negative truth of what he says, that "apart from me you can do nothing" (15:5). The text is unequivocal. Jesus is the life-source for Christians. This is why we must love him. Loving him is our connection to him, our means of staying connected to him, and one way we do battle with those things that threaten to erode our commitment to him. Without faith in and experience with Jesus we have no resurrection spirituality, leaving us with the weariness of "works righteousness."

All of this should make it clear that Christian spirituality must be rooted in the heart of the gospel, which is Jesus Christ. In short, the ends of Christian spirituality depend upon the means. Loving the way Jesus loved is a by-product of not only believing in Jesus, but trustfully loving him. In this kind of spirituality, Jesus is not simply the example for Christians to follow. He is the means of our obedience to the will of God, of our living as the people of God in our own time. Jesus was not a good man who showed Christians a better way. Our core belief is that he is God incarnate, the one in whom God has revealed divine grace and love and has declared the divine intention to be with us without our deserving it. This is why John wrote:

God's love was revealed among us in this way: God sent his only Son into the world so that we might live through him. In this is love, not that we loved God but that he loved us and sent his Son to be the atoning sacrifice for our sins (1 John 4:9–10).

Christian spirituality does not exist extraneous to Jesus. He is the particularity of Christian spirituality. He is the cornerstone of our individual and corporate life as Christians. We do not try to love others. We love him, and in the mystery of both faith and experience, we receive the power of the Holy Spirit to love the way he loved. Christians must be careful not to get the cart before the horse when it comes to spirituality. Everything is derivative of our relationship to Jesus. Everything.

As we live into this reality, what we discover is precisely what Jesus wanted Peter to know. Loving him and loving the way he loved are inseparable. The former makes the latter possible. The latter nurtures the former. In Robert Coles's conversation with Ruby Bridges, a revealing moment came when he asked her why she prayed for the people who were threatening to kill her. He said her eyes got big and she said, "Oh, doctor, don't you think they need praying for?" He asked Ruby where she had learned to pray for them. She said she had learned it from her mother and father, and from the preacher at her church. I do not think it is putting words in Ruby's mouth to say that what she had learned from her family and her church was that loving Jesus meant loving others the way he loved them. That is the heart of Christian spirituality.

In his reflections on living and working with the poor in Peru, Nouwen wrote that his experience presented him the challenge of answering the questions,

Do I really want to know Jesus? Do I really want to listen to him? Do I really want to take up my cross and follow him? Do I really want to dedicate myself to unconditional service? (Nouwen, 1983, 184)

Essentially what we have been saying is that spirituality that is Christian begins in answering Yes to these questions, and then living the Yes we give.

+ + +

All of the above has been intended to affirm the necessity of a Christological foundation for spirituality in the church. In other words, we have focused on the content of a Christian spirituality. But the "how to" questions we bracketed earlier are still before us. Even if we know what a Christian spirituality is, how does it happen? What do we do to have it? How do we come to know Jesus, to love him, and to love the way he loved?

It comes as no surprise if I say that there is no simple, or even single, answer to these questions. This is because any answer is finally rooted in the reality of the mystical (not mysterious) paradox which lies at the heart of the gospel itself. That paradox is the startling truth that we do not make a relationship with Jesus happen at all. He does! That is to say, he comes to us first, even as he came to those disciples on the Galilean seashore before and after his resurrection. He meets us. He knows us. He loves us. And that makes our meeting him, knowing him, loving him, and loving the way he loved, possible.

Yet within the context of this paradox, there are some things we can do—indeed, must do—that "position" us for this encounter. There is a diversity of ways to do this with which most of us are familiar but whose revelatory potential is easily missed. Prayer is certainly the first among them. As we shall discuss (chapter 5), praying is the process of opening ourselves to new depths in experiencing the presence of the raised Jesus. For this reason, our persistence in prayer is a reliable indicator of just how serious we are about a relationship to Jesus that moves from faith to experience. Reading and studying scripture is another way Jesus meets us. Encountering the presence of Jesus through scripture is precisely why there is scripture in the first place. The books of the Bible form the canon because early Christians experienced the continued presence of the raised Jesus in those books. Had this not been the case, they would not be scripture for the church today. Sacred moments when a verse or passage speaks deeply to mind and heart are signs that we have encountered Jesus' presence. In such moments the inspiration of scripture takes on existential meaning. We should never underestimate the power of the Bible's words to reveal the true Word to us. In an age of biblical illiteracy in the church, this way of positioning ourselves through scripture to meet, know, and come to love Jesus and his ways has never been more urgent.

A third way is through participation in corporate worship. The church gathered to worship is a community positioned to be met by the Lord of the church. The church gathered in his presence is a witness to the communal nature of Christian spirituality. The experience of the presence of Jesus in worship is one of the ways the Spirit moves us from spectatorship to discipleship. While worship in many churches today desperately needs renewal (see chapter 7), the church gathered for worship offers us a primary way to praise him, and in that praise he meets us. Praise is a response, an offering, if you will, *soli Deo gloria,* solely to the glory of God—a response to God's overflowing, self-communicating joy, to use Karl Barth's phrase. Praise requires our getting beyond our own needs and wants by focusing us on divine love. In this way praise frees us to become vulnerable to experiencing the presence of Jesus.

This is especially true in what I believe is the central act of worship, the Lord's Supper. Regardless of our theological interpretation of the bread and wine, the reality is that the presence of Jesus Christ is experienced by all who are open to it in the breaking of bread. The experience of the two disciples on the road to Emmaus (Luke 24:13–35) whose eyes were opened to the presence of Jesus in the breaking of bread was proleptic of the experience of countless others who through the ages and today have gathered around his Table of Remembrance. Perhaps at no other point in our spiritual journey do we experience being loved by the One we are called to love and serve save the act of breaking bread as a community who claim his name.

Jesus himself told us yet another way he will meet us, which is in the sharing of our lives and resources with those in need (Matthew 25:31–46). In moments when we help someone who is hungry, who is in need of clothes, who is sick or in prison, or anytime we reach out to another in need, Jesus promises us he will meet us in them. In the very act of loving the way he loved, he comes to us and strengthens our love for him.

The fact that Jesus met the disciples in unexpected ways, such as his encounter with Peter on the seashore, should suggest to us that he might come to us in unexpected ways and at unexpected times, as well. If he is raised, then there is no reason for us not to expect to be encountered unexpectedly. The issue is whether or not we will be there when he does. The ways mentioned that position us to be met by him leave us with the challenge to be there when he comes.

When someone asks me, "How do I learn to love Jesus and love the way he loved?" my response is, "Put yourself in a position of encountering his presence. Trust that he will come to you, and when he does, you will know it. And the more you put yourself in this position, the more you will grow both in loving him and loving the way he loved." But even more can be said. In the chapters to follow, our discussion explores in more detail what happens in this encounter and delves into some of the struggles that attend it.

2

SIGNS OF
SPIRITUAL
GROWTH

*We are a long way from knowing all that is involved
in the call of Christ...but we soon discover that as we
try faithfully to obey the simple calls we hear, the
ability to hear seems to grow.*

Elton Trueblood

In the previous chapter we defined the "ends" of a
Christian spirituality as loving the way Jesus loved. We also said that the
means to these ends—loving Jesus—is what makes spirituality "Christian." We concluded with identifying some ways to position ourselves
to experience the presence of Jesus. Such encounters become the points
of growth in both the "means" and "ends" of Christian spirituality.

This now brings us to the question, How do we know when we are
making progress? Are there signs that tell us we are growing in loving
Jesus with a "first loyalty" kind of love and loving the way he loved? We
have identified the goal of Christian spirituality. Are there ways to know
that we are moving toward it?

Here we need to be careful. There is a danger in measuring spiritual
progress. Spiritual growth is usually subtle and even secret, recognizable
sometimes only after lengthy periods of feeling frustrated and discouraged. Progress more often than not seems slow in the life of the Spirit.
This easily leads to harsh self-judgments that put unnecessary obstacles
in our path, when the way is already tough enough. This situation is
exacerbated by the fact that knowledge may run ahead of experience.
We may know or believe something to be true before we actually expe-

rience it as true. In other words, when it comes to the life of the Spirit, the head and the heart do not always grow concurrently. Moreover, some people unfortunately value experiential growth more than growth in knowledge and understanding. Such bifurcation of Christian spirituality misses the mark. While the mind and heart may not grow concurrently, in the end any separation of them is a false one. We are mind and heart—and soul—not one or the other.

Despite the need for caution, however, there is still value in having some sense of the spiritual progress we are making. People need to know they are on the right track, that their labors are not in vain, even in the life of the Spirit. In this chapter, therefore, I want to discuss specific ways we as Christians can recognize and affirm our growth in loving Jesus and loving the way he loved. What we will be discussing are something like "signposts" along the way that let us know where we are spiritually. It is important to keep in mind that we are not talking about "steps" to spiritual maturity. We are, rather, highlighting indicators of growth, pointers that assure us that we are going in the right direction. In short, I am not trying to *pre*-scribe how to grow spiritually. My intention is to *de*-scribe some of the ways we can recognize the growth that is taking place. Too often discussions of spirituality imply or explicitly state the "steps" to spiritual maturity. Life in general does not yield to "steps," and neither does the life of the Spirit.

This discussion, then, is about signposts, not steps, that help us know where we are and affirm the journey we are on. For this purpose I want to use the metaphor of movement to describe the signs of spiritual growth. Imagine these movements as the movements of a symphony. At times a theme will repeat itself with variations such as a round. At another time the movement will be slow, or moderate and steady. Then the pace might quicken with intensity. Movements of spiritual growth can feel this way, underscoring the freedom and flow in the life of the Spirit that is inviting, if not enticing.

The order of these spiritual movements is both random and intentional, if such a thing is possible. That is to say, they are not listed in order of importance or priority, yet it is often the case experientially that progress with one movement leads to progress in another, as well as the same effect being experienced in a negative way. Sometimes lack of movement in one area stifles movement in another. At other times we may find ourselves engaged in several movements at once, or working at one particular movement over a long period of time. We may even begin working once again with a movement with which we thought we had finished. The point is to learn to identify the movements in order to help ourselves see the ways in which we are growing.

1. FROM WORKS TO GRACE

"Works righteousness" is the deadly enemy of Christian spirituality. It is, of course, theologically wrong. Christians think Judaism is legalistic, when in truth many of us are more legalistic, if for no other reason than the fact that we do not have a history of understanding law as an expression of divine grace. Christians misinterpret Judaism when we think it is nothing but law. The tendency to become legalistic certainly exists in Judaism. The New Testament suggests that some of the conflicts Jesus had with the scribes and Pharisees were over this very point. But the irony is that many Christians have, since the time of Jesus, become just as legalistic as the religious leaders with whom Jesus was in conflict.

Growing up, I was taught that Sunday was not only a day for going to church but was a day on which a good Christian did not swim, play ball, go to movies, or in any way have "fun." Someone humorously described Puritanism as the haunting suspicion that somewhere, somebody was having fun. It is a caricature, but not without truth. Christians talk a lot about grace and mercy, but for the most part the church has taught that such grace was available only to the pure in heart, which meant the person who did and did not do what the church prescribed.

This kind of Christian faith takes the joy out of being a Christian. It turns spiritual growth into "works righteousness," a list of things to do and not to do. Conservatives and liberals have committed the same mistake in this regard. My church experience as a child was conservative. But I have heard the same "works righteousness" from liberals since then. Only the agenda is different. Conservatives are steeped in legalistic moralism. Liberals are steeped in legalistic social ministry. Conservatives tend to talk about what a good Christian ought not to do. Liberals talk about what a good Christian ought to do. Neither teaches a gospel of grace.

Spiritual growth is moving from a focus on works to a focus on grace. Spiritually mature Christians understand there is right and wrong. They know the social implications of the gospel. They know faith must be expressed in actions. They know that God judges sin and expects radical obedience. But they also understand that neither moral goodness nor social action saves or redeems. They know that Jesus is the way of grace. Even more, they know that much of the struggle they have in a personal relationship with him is believing in his grace and accepting it as true for them and not just for others. Many are the Christians, some of whom are clergy, who proclaim a gospel of grace for others, but have never really claimed it for themselves. The spiritual journey for Christians involves making the move away from the enslavement of "works righteousness" to the incredible freedom and joy that come with experiencing mercy.

This may be the most difficult of all the movements we shall discuss, so shot through is the church with "works righteousness." Christians are like all other folk in possessing an insatiable need to deserve what we get. Of course, if we did get what we deserved from God, not one of us would have any hope. But we don't think this way. Instead, we convince ourselves that we have accepted the news that we are saved by grace. Our transparency is shown in the subtle pride we take in the works we do and in the frequency with which we make judgments on the faith and faithfulness of others.

In free church traditions such as my own, lay leaders often pray at the Lord's Table. Their prayers, a colleague recently pointed out, are primarily "works righteousness" prayers. Frequently heard are the words, "Lord, make us worthy of this sacrifice." But free church traditions are not alone in this. These very words also appear in liturgical prayer books. And both miss the truth of the Table which is precisely the fact that we are not worthy, and the heart of the good news is that we do not have to be. Why? Because God's grace is sufficient. So afraid have we been that someone might abuse divine grace that we have been afraid to preach it. In the process we have committed a worse sin. We have replaced it with "works righteousness," whether it be good deeds or moral goodness. Anything that makes God's love conditional falls under the category of "works righteousness."

Growth in loving Jesus teaches us that he loves us *in spite of* rather than *because of* what we do. This kind of growth moves us closer and closer to being truly free to love the way he loved, not to gain anything, but solely to give. Here is a reliable sign of spiritual growth. More than that, this movement is the foundation for understanding the efficacy of the ones to follow.

2. FROM "LORD, BE PRESENT TO ME" TO "LORD, HELP ME BE PRESENT TO YOU"

It is interesting that we so often pray for Jesus to be present when the gospel declares that he is forever with us. The heart of our faith is the presence of God. God declares the cries of a suffering people enslaved in Egypt have been heard, and God determines to deliver them (Exodus 3:7–8); God promises to be with Moses when he returns to lead the people out of Egypt (Exodus 3:12); God promises to be with Joshua when Moses dies (Joshua 1:5); Jesus' very birth is called "Emmanuel" (Matthew 1:23); and Paul declares that nothing in life or death can separate us from the love of God in Christ Jesus (Romans 8:38–39).

It is appropriate to invoke the presence of God in the sense that the invocation of divine presence is always appropriate. The testimony of scripture, however, leads us to understand that at a deeper level God is never absent, that God is always with us. As Christians we can claim the promise of Jesus that he would always be with us (Matthew 28:20). The real issue is whether we are present to him. Spiritual growth at least includes a maturing sense of being present to the presence of the risen Lord, of looking for signs of his presence, which is forever with us.

An important sign of spiritual growth is the movement from focusing on the need for God's presence to be invoked to a focus on our being present to God. It is never a matter of God's forsaking us, but of our forsaking or neglecting God. Maintaining contact with Jesus daily, seeking to present every moment of our lives to him—this is being present to him. The more conscious we are that we are making this choice, the more mature our love for him becomes.

I have found that this movement is deceptively powerful. It seems such a small thing to say that Jesus is always present and that we need to pay attention to that presence. Yet my experience is that the impact is significant in the gathered community when all who are present are reminded that Jesus is already present and that the issue is whether they are present to him. It is a simple thing, yet something that deepens our sense of Jesus' being present to us.

3. FROM DUPLICITY TO SIMPLICITY

Sister Elaine Prevallet, SLN, defines simplicity as "having a clear focus on the one thing necessary, an undivided heart." Recalling Jesus' words that no one can serve two masters (Matthew 6:24), she writes, "He doesn't say you ought not, or you may not, but you *can* not. It isn't possible....Jesus isn't talking about how it should be, the ideal world; he is enunciating the deepest laws of life." Finally she adds: "To put it a different way, we can't become single-hearted or single-minded unless we confront our double-heartedness and double-mindedness" (Prevallet, 9).

These wise words point to the fact that loving Jesus requires disciplined commitment. Christians with a measure of mature spirituality consciously choose to make belonging to Jesus the determining factor regarding their values and relationships. The world entices us to believe in its definitions of security, power, and personal freedom. Solid growth in belonging to Jesus is taking place when we resist this temptation, declaring our freedom from cultural enslavement by the priorities we make in our lives.

A danger Christians face is not to realize just how difficult single-mindedness and single-heartedness are to live. This often happens because the choices we make are usually between good things—a child's soccer match or attending church; opening Christmas gifts or attending Christmas Eve worship; holding out to see how the monthly bills go or making a financial contribution to the church; relaxing at home after a hard day's work or attending an evening Bible study; hurrying to another task or taking time to listen to a colleague who needs to talk; taking a firm stand on a divisive issue or seeking to be open-minded toward other points of view. None of these choices, and the many others just like them, are easy precisely because each represents that which can be considered a good thing. Yet choices have to be made. There is no prescription to follow in doing so. But what can be called "creeping" duplicity is a factor not to be ignored.

One challenge single-heartedness and single-mindedness present to Christians is the call to give an account of the hope that is within us, albeit we do so in gentleness and reverence (1 Peter 3:15–16). It is not a matter of being able to make the right choice all the time. It is, instead, being willing to make a choice in humility and being open to learning from it. To do this is a good indicator of spiritual growth.

4. FROM TALKING TO LISTENING

One of the most reliable indicators of spiritual growth is when our desire to listen exceeds our need to speak. This includes talking to another person and talking to God. The world is full of words, most of which most of us could do without. But all of us make our individual contribution to the problem. In fact, the church is a place where words are used, misused, overused, and abused. The Quaker practice of speaking only when one senses being led by the Holy Spirit to do so is a practice that could have a significant influence on churches growing into spiritual maturity.

But the primary value such a practice could have is in reminding us that all words should arise from the life of the Spirit. The Christian who learns how to put this conviction into practice is one who has more spiritual depth and maturity than the vast majority of us. Perhaps the failure of Christians to be this mature was what led James to write of the power of the tongue to bless and curse with equal fervor (James 3:9–10).

A friend told me of an experience that gave him encouragement regarding his spiritual growth in this area. He and his wife had just been through a period of tension related to his relationship to her family. One morning they both awakened early. She began to describe some of the ways he was relating to her family that were contributing to the tension. She went on for about an hour. Much to his surprise, he managed to keep the lid on his impulses to defend himself. He simply let her know he was listening. Later that day he prayed about the experience, felt a sense of calm about the whole situation he had not had before, and ended with the feeling of having let go of thoughts and feelings that stood in the way of his having inner peace about it. He came to the conclusion that the key in all of this was his ability to listen rather than talk to his wife. She needed to talk. He needed to listen.

Learning to do the latter when our tendency is to do the former is a reliable sign of spiritual growth.

5. FROM HOLDING ON TO LETTING GO

"Just let go" is a familiar piece of advice today. It is common to see bumper stickers that say, "Let Go to God." While this kind of thing may trivialize "letting go" in life, it does not negate the wisdom of doing it. The image of an elderly woman with fists tightly clenched gradually opening her hands can be a useful metaphor for prayer (Nouwen, 1972). It is also a metaphor of life. Spiritual maturity can be described as moving from living life with clenched fists to living life with open hands. We cling to things we are better off letting go of. Holding on to old wounds, holding on to children when it is time to let them go, holding on rather than celebrating love relationships, all these are signs of spiritual immaturity. Spiritual growth means developing the will to let go when the time for letting go has come. Spiritual growth creates the inner freedom that forms the foundation for living without clinging, for loving without possessing or being possessed.

Being able to "let go" is an important benchmark of spiritual maturity. It is a sign that we understand the folly of trying to control circumstances and people. Letting go means being able to trust that our lives are ultimately sustained by faith rather than control. It shows we have decided to live out of love rather than fear. For Christians, spiritual maturity means living so close to Jesus that his love replaces the grip fear has on us. So much of life can be ruled by fear, which is the root of such things as prejudice, anxiety, bitterness, resistance to change. In a crisis we sometimes open ourselves to divine love and in the process are released from the power fear holds over us. Maturity in the Spirit is moving to that inward place where we live this way all the time.

6. FROM FEAR TO FREEDOM

Speaking of fear, one of the promises mature Christians experience as true is that divine love casts out fear (1 John 4:18). It fills us so perfectly, so completely, that fear is squeezed out, producing an incredible sense of inward freedom. Ironically, fear is at the root of the kind of judgmentalism that has characterized and continues to characterize religious zeal. When we are afraid, we are unable to respond to others with understanding, which leads to the common problem of seeing the speck in another's eye while missing the plank in our own. It is missing the plank in our own eye that is the real problem spiritually. One of the first fruits of divine love replacing fear in a person's heart is having the inner strength to see ourselves for what we—and everyone else—are—sinners. Owning our sins makes it less likely that we will focus on the sins of another. This is not to say that we tolerate anything and everything. What we are talking about is attitude. Making judgments about the behavior and performance of others is a part of life. What saves us from falling into judgmentalism is humility.

Divine love makes humility possible. A fearful heart has no room for humility. It is too busy trying to prove its own worth. A heart filled with love knows it does not have to earn a place in God's heart, or in the heart of others. This kind of freedom allows room for accepting our humanness without fear; to know that we need the forgiveness of others, not because we are without worth, but because we have feet of clay. A heart ruled by divine love is free to pay attention to the impulse to be a person who forgives rather than judges. The difference is subtle, but significant. We may make judgements, but we do so reluctantly and for the purpose of redemption rather than condemnation. Love makes this possible precisely because it has released us from the hold fear can have on us. Knowing this kind of divine love is another reliable sign of spiritual growth.

7. FROM ALIENATION TO FORGIVENESS

Every Christian knows about the need for forgiveness, and the need to be forgiving. But it takes genuine spiritual maturity to receive the one and to give the other. The Christian life begins, of course, in forgiveness. Divine love and grace have meaning because we are a forgiven people. At the same time, forgiveness lies at the heart of loving others the way Jesus loved them, as Ruby Bridges demonstrated. Forgiveness is always in the heart of spiritually mature Christians.

Yet there is perhaps no issue with which Christians struggle more than being able to forgive. Whether it is in families, the church, or the larger society, Christians often cling to alienation rather than being forgiving. We nurse anger and hurt for all they are worth, making the process of forgiving slow at best. That it should not be this way seems to do little to prevent it. Yet not one of us would have the relationships that mean so much to us had we ourselves not been the recipients of forgiveness from others. Sadly, we refuse to give what we desperately need.

Spiritual maturity means forgiving others, while withholding forgiveness is a telling sign of spiritual immaturity. The key to having the capacity to forgive is the degree to which we are connected to Jesus, love him, and seek to belong to him first in our lives. We cannot fool ourselves. We know an unforgiving spirit contradicts discipleship. The maturity level of our love for Jesus shows itself quite clearly in whether or not we are quick to forgive, refuse to nurse anger and hurt, and are unwilling to live alienated from others. Moving toward forgiveness offers a reliable measure of spiritual growth and development.

8. From Doing to Being

There is a place for action in the life of the Spirit, as we shall discuss later. But there is also a place for learning how just to be, to claim value as a child of God solely because we belong to Jesus and not because of anything we are doing. In modern American society, recognition is given to what a person does. But in the final analysis people respond more to who a person is rather than what a person does. "Being" is the foundation for community life in the church, not "doing." Balance is needed between the two, but today the weight is on the side of action, not being. It is well and good if actions spring from character, but they can never be a substitute for it. Who we are matters. Not just what we do. It is a message not easily grasped by a world that measures worth by one's productivity but a message without which not one person can be whole.

A creative book of some years ago that presented the gospel in new images contains the story of "The Porcupine Whose Name Didn't Matter." Joggi had always been cautious, given the way the other animals kept their distance because of the prickly spines sticking out all over him. Now and then someone might say hello, but that was about it. To protect himself from the pain of his isolation, when someone asked his name, Joggi would reply abruptly, "It doesn't matter! It doesn't matter what my name is! Can't you see? What difference does it make? I won't tell you what my name is, because it doesn't matter." It was his way of making sure he did not let himself become hopeful of someone befriending him even for a moment and then experiencing the disappointment of their walking away.

Life was this way until Joggi came across Gamiel, a raccoon near death from a gunshot wound. Gamiel was blinded by the shot that had ripped part of his face off. He limped badly. Gamiel was lying helpless and afraid when Joggi's appearance startled him. It took some maneuvering on both their parts, but it wasn't long before these two isolated and needy souls came to be friends. They made a kind of home for each other, like a shelter from excessive pain each of them had known. But Joggi remained obstinent about not telling Gamiel his name. It still didn't matter, he said, trying to mask his fear that even the wounded raccoon would finally leave him.

Gamiel didn't force the issue, and the two of them stayed together one full year before the end came for Gamiel. For a long time Joggi stood silent beside the body of his friend. Finally he cleared his throat and began to speak:

> You know, I've been expecting this for quite some time now...I never expected you to live this long. And yet...well, I hoped that it might have been a little longer. Do you know what I mean? You see, I never knew anybody very well before...but I felt like I knew you...even without talking. I have a really hard time talking to anybody or getting to know anybody...I hope you don't mind my talking so much...I suppose it's just that I had a little more to tell you before you died...I've been wanting to tell you that it has been an honor to meet you, and that you are indeed a handsome raccoon, and that I would like to consider you my friend...and by the way, I'd like to tell you what my name is...It's Joggi. (Bell, 118-120)

The truth is, Joggi's name did matter! It mattered because who he was mattered. That is what this story is about—*being*, about the need for everyone of us to recognize our worth as persons. It is the gospel couched in a story about the mystical meeting between two wounded creatures who needed each other and discovered how much each of them was worth in their becoming friends. The story tells us what the gospel tells us, that in the encounter with the One who loves us perfectly we discover the truth about ourselves, that before and after anything we do, we have worth in who we are. In hearing this good news, we begin the journey of learning how to love him, others—and ourselves.

9. FROM HANDSHAKES TO HUGS

A handshake carries the image of greeting another with friendliness, while maintaining one's distance, preventing another from getting too close, as if they are invading our private space. All of us at times need such space. But intimacy between ourselves and God, others, or creation cannot deepen as long as we keep them at arm's length. The handshake is to live in a relationship from a safe distance, conveying a hesitancy to trust ourselves to another.

A hug, on the other hand, has the image of appropriate intimacy. To hug is to allow another into our private space, perhaps not to stay, but at least to visit. We are not talking about a physical hug so much as an attitude with which we view relationships. The hug symbolizes a desire to be close to another, even to be vulnerable to another. It places trust in intimacy rather than distance.

A sign of spiritual growth is moving from the need for distance toward greater intimacy and trust of God, others, and the world around us. This kind of inner movement suggests growing in one's willingness to be open and honest with God, to engage the world as Jesus did, to love with abandonment and joy. This is not to be naive, but to be willing to take risks rather than always playing it safe. It shows a willingness to be stretched beyond our comfort zone to see what new thing Jesus is teaching us.

Too often Christians accept their present capacity for intimacy by saying, "It's who I am." The flaw in this statement is that the status quo can always be justified in this way. My native Virginia would still be maintaining segregation as public policy based on this kind of thinking. Who we are does not prohibit growth. Indeed, constitutive to who we are is the capacity to change and grow. Intimacy as an attitude is possible for everyone. And for the Christian it begins in a personal relationship to Jesus Christ. The more secure we become in this relationship, the more willing we become to move from an attitude of handshakes to an attitude of hugs in all relationships.

10. FROM BEING RESPONSIBLE FOR TO BEING RESPONSIBLE TO

A spiritually mature Christian learns how to distinguish between being a care-taker and being a care-giver. The latter means being responsible to them. It means sharing the load, showing concern, while at the same time being able to keep one's distance and respect boundaries of responsibility. Trying to be responsible for others, on the other hand, is unhealthy for the care-taker and the recipient. It involves our taking responsibility for other people. Care-taking perpetuates needy relationships. It makes growing up more difficult for persons who struggle with taking responsibility for themselves. Dependency becomes the linchpin in such relationships. One needs to be needed; the other needs to be helped. Both people are living through their needs rather than exercising personal will.

Loving Jesus leads Christians into self-reflection that forces us to examine our motivation for helping others. Living close to Jesus fills us with his love, evokes our love for him, and frees us to love others because of their needs rather than our own. It also provides us with sufficient personal security that we are not held in bondage to the need to be needed. This makes us strong enough to love without being manipulated, strong enough to love others without smothering them or taking responsibility for them. In short, we are free to become care-givers. Sensing this is happening in us is a reliable sign that we are growing spiritually.

11. FROM INDIVIDUALISM TO COMMUNITY

Individualism is a trademark of American society. It has been the driving force behind many accomplishments. Its virtues have been eloquently extolled by the likes of Emerson and Thoreau. And its role as the vehicle for the human spirit has been confirmed through events such as the collapse of Soviet communism. Individual liberty was a founding principle of American democracy, as the early leaders of our nation reacted against the tyranny of European despotism and class privilege. Our self-identity is a nation of people who practice the ethic of self-reliance. Picking ourselves up by our own bootstraps is thought to be virtuous, even a sign of the blessing of God.

In this kind of environment, concern for community is easily neglected. We think in individualistic terms so much that it seems to be second nature to us. Yet spiritually mature Christians know that the virtues of individualism must be balanced with the communal claims of the gospel. Jesus answered Abel's question, "Am I my brother's keeper?" with the parable of the Good Samaritan, with his affirmation of the inseparable nature of love for God and love for neighbor, and his commitment to healing the sick and lame. God did not call a person, but a people in forming a nation, and Jesus is the head of the body of Christ, not just a leader of individuals.

Commitment to being in community with others is a growing edge for Christians. When the well-being of a neighbor becomes as important as one's own well-being, we can be sure that we have moved to a deeper level of experience with Jesus. Moreover, working for a sense of community among all peoples is a tangible way Christians can contribute to a better world. Mature Christians seek to model community among themselves as a symbol of the future God is creating, as well as a witness to the way in which we can keep from destroying this planet. Indeed, the breakdown of community responsibility signals a serious change in our society, a change not for the better. A century ago the French writer, de Tocqueville, pointed to an internal cohesiveness that transcended individualism as the key to the survival of the new American democracy he came here to observe. We have not heeded his counsel. The effects of excessive individualism have been documented (Bellah, 1985). We have reached the point where individualism often runs roughshod over the good of the whole. Spiritual growth is the movement from excessive individualism to a commitment to promoting the health and well-being of the community. This is never done at the expense of the individual, but out of concern for all the members of the church. The whole is as important as the parts in a spiritually mature church.

I believe this is the kind of church where members seek to open themselves to the power of the Holy Spirit. Because they do they become a church in which the members "are always called to *become more*"

(Vanier, 23), more than they are individually and more than they are collectively. Perfection is not the goal. Rather, the goal is to be as fully human as they can be within the context of a community that trusts forgiveness is stronger than alienation, and love stronger than sin. In this kind of church the members can truly belong to one another because they trust that in Jesus they are collectively as the church more than any one of them can be alone.

12. FROM COMPETITION TO COMPASSION

American society thrives on competition. It's the free market way. Most Americans believe that competition makes people do their best. Athletics has become a national symbol of our way of life. Compete, struggle, fight, win. These are the values we prize, whether it relates to a spelling bee or the Super Bowl.

The problem with competition, of course, is that it thrives on adversarial relationships. There has to be a protagonist and an antagonist. Most of the time adversaries put aside their differences at the end of the competition. Not always. Rivalries can become so embittered that fights and riots break out. Opposing softball teams in church-sponsored leagues frequently get into arguments to the point of coming to blows. Sometimes the drive to win leads people into criminal behavior. Tanya Harding wanted to win the national ice skating championship so badly that she conspired to have her primary competitor, Nancy Kerrigan, assaulted. French Tennis star, Monica Seles, was stabbed in the back by a fan of Steffi Graf, her German competitor. Businesses seek to undercut competitors or suppress damaging information about their products, even when public safety is put in jeopardy.

These are examples of the extreme, of course. But they point to the fact that competition often creates an attitude that makes winning, as legendary football coach Vince Lombardy put it, "the only thing." In this kind of culture, compassion, the will to stand with and to understand another, finds little nurture or support. The weak can be trampled or derided for not being able to keep up with the pack. Injustice is dismissed on the basis of personal failure to rise above circumstances.

Growth in loving the way Jesus loved involves having one's eyes opened regarding the tension between competition and compassion. It is easy for Christians to get caught up in an environment of competition to the point of not being advocates of compassion, to the point of hardening our hearts to injustices that overwhelm others. "Bleeding heart liberals" is the label often given spiritually mature Christians who seek to live a life of compassion in a competitive society. While the label is intended to be derogatory, the image of one's heart bleeding because of the pain of another is appropriate for those who desire to love the way Jesus loved in a world that refuses to recognize how hardened its heart is to those who are unable to compete, or those for whom the "playing field" is not level.

We can be sure we are growing in Christlike love when our first response to the plight of others is unconditional compassion. Spiritual maturity always makes Christians more willing to err on the side of mercy, to err in helping the undeserving in order to avoid failing to respond to one in genuine need. Jesus did not seem to be concerned with distributing compassion on the basis of merit or achievement, but in making sure that everyone knew they were loved and cared for. We can trust that growing in our capacity to love him will produce the fruit of having the same concern. Years ago I read an intriguing account of a little league soccer game. The article described the play as intense. At one point a player was injured, and members of both teams ran to help. This kind of attitude seemed to mark the play of all the players throughout the match. At the end of the game, the article said, the players looked exhausted, and only then did the teams ask anyone what the score was. During the entire time of play the focus had been on the game, the sport being enjoyed by both sides. The score was immaterial.

What a marvelous parable for today. Spiritually mature Christians are people who are moving from competition in which scores are kept and winning is everything to a place where the values by which they live are care and compassion.

13. FROM INDEPENDENCE TO INTERDEPENDENCE

One of the helpful insights in Stephen Covey's book, *The Seven Habits of Highly Effective People*, is his juxtaposition of "dependence" at the bottom of the pyramid of personal growth, "independence" in the middle, and "interdependence" at the top. The seven habits he discusses lead a person to move from one to the other. Independence is the goal, which is the by-product of balancing one's physical, spiritual, mental, and social/emotional needs. In business terms, he calls this the balance between "production" of desired results and "production capacity," or what produces the results. Spiritually this balance is knowing that our lives are intertwined with the lives of others, that all of us are bound together in a relationship of mutual dependence, i.e., interdependence.

Jesus lived the life of one who chose to bind himself to others. If any word describes the nature of the relationship he wanted all people to share, it is "interdependence," not out of necessity but out of choice, a choice dictated by love. Spiritual growth means growing so close to him that we choose to bind ourselves to others interdependently. This is a free choice that arises from faith in the oneness of God and an awareness of our shared humanity. Christians who express interdependence through attitudes and actions have made a significant movement in spiritual development. They have learned how to balance being right with being mutually supportive, how to balance commitment to principles with commitment to people. They recognize that interdependence means learning how to compromise for the common good and maintain one's personal integrity. They are committed to working toward win/win situations rather than being content with win/lose. They know no one has a corner on truth, that all people are sinful, and that living together with any degree of harmony tests the spiritual maturity of all Christians.

A significant and tangible expression of interdependence is an attitude of inclusivity. This means having the will to work at welcoming a diversity of persons, ideas, and viewpoints. This kind of open mind and open heart is the by-product of the sense of connectedness with others interdependence creates. It cannot be any other way. Exclusive interdependence is an oxymoron. By nature genuine interdependence creates inclusiveness and celebrates diversity. Spiritual maturity is a recognition that God is the author of diversity. This affirmation empowers us to receive the gift of diversity without fear. It is a good sign that we have moved from independence to interdependence.

14. FROM MIND VERSUS HEART TO MIND AND HEART

A very important sign of spiritual growth and maturity is the rejection of anti-intellectualism that pits the mind against the heart. Jesus spoke of loving God with the mind as well as the heart (Matthew 22:37; Mark 12:30; Luke 10:27). But the church's tendency through the centuries to view science as a threat to faith has fostered an unhealthy anti-intellectualism that causes people to believe they have to choose heart over mind to follow Jesus. As a consequence, many Christians are suspicious of intellectual pursuit as a vocation of faith. They believe faith is a matter of feeling only, as if spirituality has nothing to do with the mind. Mature Christians know this is not true. Faith can be clearheaded as well as heartfelt. Thoughts and feelings together create a balance essential in spiritual development.

The Bible counsels Christians to think as well as believe. 1 Peter 3:15 declares: "Always be ready to make your defense to anyone who demands from you an accounting for the hope that is in you; yet do it with gentleness and reverence." This is as much about spiritual maturity as it is about witnessing. Faith consists of both trust and understanding. Loving Jesus and loving the way he loved involve solid thinking as much as heartfelt devotion. Love is more than a feeling, just as understanding is more than comprehension. Being able to account for the hope that is within as Christians does not mean having to choose between mind and heart. Instead, both are needed in order to make a credible witness. Spiritually mature Christians know they do not have to park their brains outside the church to be people of faith. Spirituality is not about choosing heart over mind. It's about becoming whole persons, loving Jesus, and loving the way he loved with mind, heart, and soul.

15. FROM BEING TO DOING

We have already mentioned the need to value being, to grow as persons without allowing our worth to be measured solely by what we do. This is an important emphasis. Yet what we do is also a reliable indicator of the degree to which we both love Jesus and love the way he loved. There is no escape from the admonishment in the letter of James to "be doers of the word, and not merely hearers" (1:22). Faith involves action or it is not faith. Loving Jesus translates into loving the way he loved if it truly marks what we believe and have experienced. It is not possible truly to love Jesus and not love another. It is not possible to claim to love the way he loved and remain passive in a world needing effective ministry. What we are talking about is balance. Prayer and action are two sides of the same coin. Contemplation issues into action. This is what loving Jesus and loving the way he loved is all about. One cannot exist without the other and be real. A sign of spiritual maturity is not simply realizing the need for balance between prayer and action, but experiencing spiritual "dizziness" when the balance is not present. This means feeling in the depths of one's soul a lack of harmony in the relationships with God, self, others, and creation. While perfect balance between prayer and action may not be possible, reasonable balance is. Attaining this kind of balance is more than a sign of spiritual growth. It is an indispensable one. The integrity of faith requires it. Living close to Jesus makes it possible. This is why Thomas Merton wrote:

> We do not go into the desert to escape people but to learn how to find them; we do not leave them in order to have nothing more to do with them, but to find out the way to do them the most good. (Merton, 1961, 80)

16. FROM WEARINESS TO JOY

Jesus said that everything he told us was for one purpose—that we might be filled with joy and that his own joy might be in us (John 15:11). It would seem that spiritual growth would at least mean becoming a person of joy. The word Jesus used for *joy*—"chara"—has the same root as *grace*—"charis." The implication is that a person of grace will be a person of joy. Experientially, this turns out to be true. Living with an attitude of grace makes life joyful. People who show no grace, no understanding, no flexibility with others are usually people who have very little joy. At the very least it is true that people who are understanding and gracious are people who have found a profound joy in living. They don't carry life around. They live it as fully as is humanly possible.

Being a person of joy does not mean refusing to face the hard realities of life. It does not mean pretending things are better than they are. Joy does not require a "Pollyanna" faith that ignores the problems of life. It means, instead, having a deep sense that one's ultimate security lies in God and nothing else. It means this life is viewed realistically, where the powers and principalities of this age are recognized for what they are—temporal but never ultimate. As strange as it may sound to contemporary ears, spiritual maturity leads to joy because of one's ability to live eschatologically. Eschatology does not mean living for the end of time. It means living with a realistic appreciation for the limitations of now. It means keeping today in perspective, recognizing that any contemporary word is never the last word because God has the last word, and that last word is Jesus.

Ironically, it takes this kind of perspective to free us to live fully in this world. Christians whose joy is rooted in a strong sense of the ultimate hope Jesus reveals are people who have the inner strength to confront social needs. These are the people who don't give up in frustration and anger. They do not lose joy precisely because it does not depend upon the immediate situation. Such spiritually mature Christians can be counted on to work for peace and justice. They know that joy is not possible if one's hopes rest on today's expectations. They are clear about the fact that genuine hope in today's world is only found in God, who is forever and forever. That hope is the only basis for joy there is.

The Christian who is able to trust the words of Jesus that the true treasures in life are not earthly things but heavenly things (Matthew 6:19–21) is the Christian whose spiritual life has reached a depth of joy no one can take away. This is the kind of joy Jesus promises he will give us. Experiencing it is a reliable sign that we are growing in loving him and loving the way he loved.

These, then, are some of the signs that reveal the extent to which we are growing in loving Jesus and loving the way he loved. If we keep in mind the caution that Christians need not spend a lot of time taking their spiritual temperatures, these signs suggest ways we can discern the growth that is taking place.

3

THE WORK OF THE HOLY SPIRIT

To live "in Christ" is to live in a mystery equal
to that of the Incarnation....this spiritual
union...is the work of the Holy Spirit, the Spirit
of Love, the Spirit of Christ.

Thomas Merton

There is a core principle related to the spiritual life
about which we need to be very clear. It is so basic that if we do not
"get" this, we miss the whole point of everything else we are saying
about Christian spirituality. This principle expands the discussion at
the end of chapter 1, where I suggested that we do not make a relationship with Jesus happen; he does. The principle is this: Christian spirituality is ultimately the work and fruit of the Holy Spirit. When Paul
asserts that "no one can say 'Jesus is Lord' except by the Holy Spirit"
(1 Corinthians 12:3), he identifies that which is also true about loving
Jesus and loving the way Jesus loved. No one can love Jesus except by
the Holy Spirit. No one can love the way Jesus loved except by the Holy
Spirit. This is the paradox of grace. Christian faith is both a gift from
God and a human response to Jesus.

Wading into a discussion of the Holy Spirit is risky. Questions immediately come to mind whenever the Holy Spirit is mentioned, such
as, "Who is the Holy Spirit?" and "What is the Spirit's relationship to
Jesus?" Such questions, of course, have to do with the mystery of the
Holy Trinity, something beyond the scope of this work. Paul's statement to the church at Corinth about the way one confesses Jesus as
Lord was a faith affirmation. He was not trying to explain the relation-

ship between Jesus and the Holy Spirit. He was simply saying they were inseparable, and that faith itself is the work of the Holy Spirit.

I am making a similar faith statement regarding the Holy Spirit and Christian spirituality. The kind of love relationship we can have with Jesus is not of our own doing. It is because of the work of the Holy Spirit that we can love Jesus and love the way Jesus loved. Thus, Christian spirituality roots itself in the affirmation of the reality of the three members of the Holy Trinity—God, Son, Spirit. The church has described this work of the Holy Spirit as justification (faith) and sanctification (spirituality). It is a helpful way to think about the Spirit's function in our lives.

More than believing in the work of the Holy Spirit, however, is the desire to emphasize the reality of actually experiencing the Spirit's work. There are various ways to describe the work of the Holy Spirit. For our purposes we will consider this work using two categories: *transformation* and *formation*. These two ways of understanding the work of the Holy Spirit in Christian spirituality are at the same time distinct and inseparable.

TRANSFORMATION

Why transformation first? This is an important question because it goes to the core of the role the Spirit plays in Christian spirituality. To speak of transformation is to acknowledge God acts first. We play a decisive role in formation. Transformation, however, is the effect of God's initiative apart from human response. Something happens to us in transformation, not because of us, but because of God. It is sometimes the case that something happens to us in spite of ourselves. Paul's conversion experience on the Damascus road (Acts 9:1–9) is a case in point. Paul was seeking Christians. He was not seeking to become a Christian. Yet that is precisely what happened to him.

This is the way it often is when it comes to the transformative work of the Holy Spirit. Something happens to a person without that person seeking it or even wanting it. The call to ministry, lay or clergy, seems this way for many. It is a call that comes without being sought and may feel like an unwelcome intrusion into a settled life. Yet it comes nonetheless. It may be a dramatic moment or it may be a moment that has evolved over several years. In either case, it is a life-changing experience that happens to a person, rather than an experience that is sought.

To begin with transformation is a way of naming up-front the role of the Holy Spirit in Christian spirituality. Here again our concern is to avoid the pitfall of "works righteousness." We have emphasized, and will continue to do so, the role Christians play in spiritual nurture and growth. But it is precisely the tendency among modern Christians, especially here in this country, to focus on human initiative that requires special care in highlighting the role of the Holy Spirit. Formation is where we have a role to play. But the transformative work of the Holy Spirit is the building block upon which formation rests. Thus we begin with attention to transformation.

Transformation is not a subject easy to understand or explain, or even to describe, primarily because it goes to the heart of the mystery of God's incarnation in Jesus Christ. Changes in us that occur in transformative moments have their roots in the life, death, and resurrection of Jesus. Further, transformation effects significant formation through information that would not be possible apart from it. The story of Jesus' conversation with Nicodemus (John 3:1–15) is an example of the distinctive and interrelated relationship of the two stages.

Nicodemus went to Jesus one evening to get more information about who he was. By his own admission, he had come to the conclusion that Jesus had been sent by God and had the power of God with him because of the "signs" or miracles he had been doing (3:2). Jesus' immediate response to Nicodemus' desire to have more information was to tell him that he would not understand what he was seeing or hearing, i.e., "see the kingdom of God," unless and until he had been born again, literally "born from above" (3:3). The "new birth" metaphor Jesus used with Nicodemus was language describing the transformative work of the Holy Spirit. Jesus went on to say that transformation is mystery that is real, just as the wind is mystery that is real (3:7–8). Moreover, transformation was the missing stage in Nicodemus' experience that was preventing information or knowledge about Jesus from becoming formative in his life. This is the point in the conversation that speaks directly to our discussion. The process of being formed through the experience of allowing information to influence us is intimately tied to the Spirit's work of transformation.

This conversation between Jesus and Nicodemus underscores the fact that transformation is no small thing. It is radical business. The apostle Paul had something to say about the radical nature of transformation when he wrote: "Do not be conformed to this world, but be transformed by the renewing of your minds" (Romans 12:2). The Greek word in the text for "transformation" is "metamorphosis." The apostle was not talking about a minor change. He was saying that "metamorphosis" was the best way to describe the radical difference being a Christian made in one's relationship to the world. No longer would the world shape and form one's life. The Spirit's transformative power makes us a different person, as if we had been born again.

FORMATION

Transformation opens the way for the work we do in forming our minds and hearts into persons who love Jesus and love the way he loved. When it is understood holistically, Christian spirituality challenges Christians to attend to their spiritual life as a process of formation. Information is the primary tool by which this is done. It is the instrument through which formation happens. Formation occurs as information makes a permanent impact on a person's life. Transformation is not the only experience involved in spiritual growth. Information plays a decisive role as well. Students, for example, have to learn when they study spirituality that a class in Bible, theology, or church history also holds the potential for spiritual nurture. When I entered seminary, a new and exciting world opened to me as I studied these subjects. Information became a source of amazing spiritual growth and development as I allowed what I was learning to shape and form me. I look back on those days as a gift of divine grace. Mind and heart were expanded and opened, providing a marvelous and refreshing foundation for my life in Jesus Christ.

Knowledge and understanding are the gifts of God to God's people when we consciously seek to be formed in the image of Christ. From the Bible, to great theologians, to contemporary writers on spirituality and church life, to secular writers who speak with wisdom about life and relationships, Christians have found much help in loving Jesus and loving the way Jesus loved when they have opened themselves to the formative power of information. A specific example of this is prints of the world's great art that hang on the walls of our main seminary building. They express the gospel in ways that inspire and help form Christians into spiritually deep persons. This is spiritual food that nurtures anyone who is open to its potential.

Formation nurtures Christians in their "first-loyalty" love relationship to Jesus and in loving others the way Jesus loved. The key, of course, lies in the way in which we approach knowledge. Knowledge does not necessarily produce virtue, but knowledge is foundational to Christian living when we allow it to be. Perhaps this is why Saint Anselm, an early church theologian, described theology as faith seeking understanding.

What I am saying is that formation is the process of allowing information—knowledge—to influence our attitudes and actions, or significantly impact our minds and hearts. At the moment when information begins to strengthen our faith, we are being formed. When our faith deepens our love relationship to Jesus and others, we are being formed. Christian spirituality is a conscious process of using information to form our relationship with Jesus, which in turn forms our relationships with others and the whole of creation. Simply put, formation is our willingness to let information make a difference in the way we think, believe, act, and relate. Values are often altered. Points of view are changed. We see things differently, and act accordingly. The information that forms us might come through study or personal experience, but the net effect is that in some measure it makes us a different person.

Reflecting once again on my seminary experience, I now know that knowledge began to free me from the anti-intellectualism I learned in my home church. Within the context of this freedom, my spirit was positioned for growth. Truth no longer loomed as a threat but became a source of hope and excitement. As a result, my capacity to love Jesus and love the way Jesus loved was far greater than it had been.

It is in the process of experiencing formation that we discover the joy learning can be. This is true in all dimensions of life and certainly ought to be true regarding our spiritual life. Knowledge forms us, changes us, renews us, as the apostle Paul said it could in Romans 12:2 mentioned previously: "be transformed by the renewing of your minds." It can inspire and expand us in ways we never dreamed possible. The joy of Christian growth is when we know that what we are learning is making a difference in our spiritual life. Whenever we allow it to happen, information can form us into persons who are more committed to a "first-loyalty" love for Jesus and to loving the way he loved.

+ + +

Transformation and formation. These words describe both the work of the Holy Spirit and ours as we grow into spiritually mature Christians. Transformation and formation are not prescriptive. They are not molds into which we must pour ourselves in order to be spiritually mature. They are descriptions of what have been and continue to be experiences common to many who walk the journey of the spiritual life. The goal is to learn better and better how to love Jesus and to love the way he loved. The process is transformative and formative. Information is a friend and facilitator of this process. Taken together, these experiences invite us into both opening ourselves to the Holy Spirit and taking responsibility for ourselves spiritually.

It may be that transformation and formation capture the paradox of Paul's curious statement in Philippians to "work out your own salvation with fear and trembling" (Philippians 2:12). Out of context these words sound like a call to "works righteousness," to saving ourselves. When understood, however, within the context of the transformative power of the Holy Spirit, they call us to the spiritual work only we can do for ourselves. Jesus does not make us love him or love the way he loved. Instead he asks us to give him "first-loyalty" love. The choice to do so is ours. In choosing to love him we experience the paradox of grace, wherein the power to love the way he loved is given to us. It is a power we do not possess on our own. At the same time, our openness to using information to form our spiritual life plays an important role in the effect the Spirit's transformative power has on us. Thus, the spiritual life involves "salvation" work we have to do for ourselves yet is ever dependent upon the Holy Spirit's power to transform our efforts into growth and maturity.

4

THE NEED
FOR DISCIPLINE

*A mark of the spiritually advanced is
their awareness of their own
laziness....Spiritual growth is effortful.*

Scott Peck

Discussions of spirituality usually center on what
is called the practice of "spiritual disciplines." Many contemporary writers
(see the Bibliography) have opened this world of classical Christian disciplines to the Protestant community that heretofore had been largely
unaware of their longtime practice in the Roman Catholic and Eastern
Orthodox traditions. Spiritual disciplines are a way for us to put
ourselves in a position of experiencing spiritual transformation and formation. They are the "tools" we use to do the work we have to do in
order to grow and be nurtured toward spiritual maturity.

There is no need to repeat here what others have said about disciplines. The particular focus of this chapter, therefore, centers around a
related issue, which is the matter of *discipline*. This is a subject generally
ignored or only briefly mentioned in most books on spirituality, a serious omission. As edifying as disciplines can be, they are very hard work.
This fact makes the issue of discipline central to the spiritual life. Spiritual disciplines work only if they are worked. That takes discipline.

One way to understand the relationship between disciplines and
discipline is think of disciplines as the work we do in spirituality. Discipline is getting up to go to work. This is not to say that God cannot and
does not break through human laziness and outright resistance to

divine love. It is only to say that Christians have a role to play in nurturing their capacity to love Jesus and to bear the cross of loving the way Jesus loved, and that work requires discipline. While disciplines may be described as the key to the door of spiritual nurture and growth, discipline is the ability to turn the key. Yet discipline is a factor largely ignored in discussions on Christian spirituality. Rather than ignore it, discipline itself deserves "disciplined" attention.

The basic question with which to begin is why being disciplined is so hard for most of us. That it is seems hardly debatable. We manifest a lack of discipline in most areas of human existence. Despite, for example, all the emphasis on physical exercise, study after study confirms that as a people we continue to be out-of-shape and overweight. The men and women we see jogging as we drive by them are exceptions rather than the rule. Most Americans are sedentary rather than active. Why? Because we do not have the discipline to work at getting and staying in shape physically.

The same thing is true for Christians in regard to our spiritual health and well-being. We are basically "out of shape" because of a lack of discipline. Yet, more emphasis has been placed on the value of Christian disciplines in the last several years than at any time in this century. Even when we do enough to acquire information about spiritual disciplines, we remain inattentive to them. This is why more information about Christian disciplines is not what most of us need.

In the many years I have been teaching spiritual formation, both in the academic environment and in the church, I have found that the common struggle is discipline. To be more precise, it is a lack of discipline. Statements such as "I just don't have the kind of time I wish I had to pray," and "I start out fine, but after a while I find it harder and harder to pray with any regularity," grow out of the struggle with discipline. On the face of it the basic problem seems to be a matter of commitment. The level of our commitment to spiritual growth determines the degree to which we are disciplined in working at it. While there is truth to this way of thinking, it fails to appreciate the multidimensional nature of commitment.

I want to suggest that commitment has three dimensions that need to be understood in order for us to have any significant degree of it. It is around these dimensions that we can organize our discussion of the problem of discipline in regard to the spiritual life. They are: Wish—Want—Will. Let us examine each of these and their relationship to one another.

The first step toward being disciplined in our spiritual development is to wish for something more than we have. A wish reflects an interest in going beyond where we are spiritually. It is the moment we begin to see new possibilities for our lives. Our curiosity is piqued. We are not ready to make any changes in our lives, but a wish for something more signals that we are no longer satisfied with the status quo.

Wishing means standing in front of a wishing well and casting a coin into it as we make a wish. This image suggests that we are not ready to do anything more than make a wish. We are not willing to accept responsibility for doing anything else. Making a wish always leaves the next step to something or someone other than ourselves. In spite of the fact that wishing does not make "it" so, it is at least a small step in the right direction spiritually. It is a sign that we know there is more to a relationship to Jesus than our present experience.

The second step is moving from wishing to wanting. When this happens, interest moves to desire. We begin to "hunger and thirst" for a deeper relationship to Jesus. Spiritual growth moves higher up our ladder of priorities. We are now ready to do what Jesus invites us to do—to ask, to seek, to knock. At this moment spiritual disciplines are recognized as tools for growth. People who want to love Jesus and love the way he loved begin to take time for prayer. They are on the journey. They want to be more than church members. Discipleship is now the goal.

Wanting a relationship to Jesus signals an awareness that simply wishing for it does not make it happen. Wanting leads to a commitment to taking personal responsibility for moving beyond knowing about Jesus to knowing him. We accept the fact that no one can make us grow spiritually. This is a crucial step. I have students who wish they would get an "A" in class, but those who do get the "A" are the ones who realize they have to want it enough to do the work required to get it. The others remain undisciplined. Wanting is the point at which discipline is seen as the prerequisite to reaching the goal.

One fruit of reaching the point of wanting to grow spiritually is that we begin to have focus in the spiritual life. That focus can be described in various ways. I think the apostle Paul clarifies one way to think about it in the passage from Romans to which we have previously made reference. Earlier we discussed Romans 12:2. Now we turn to 12:1. Together these two verses form what may be the most compelling challenge found in Paul's letters. In 12:1 he writes:

> I appeal to you therefore, brothers and sisters, by the mercies of God, to present your bodies as a living sacrifice, holy and acceptable to God, which is your spiritual worship.

Paul speaks first of the mercy of God. This is where the divine/human relationship begins—in the mercy of God. God is more than just. God is gracious. In Jesus Christ, Christians find God's grace incarnate. We cannot miss the word the incarnation speaks, if we have ears to hear. God is merciful. God is gracious. God comes to us before we ever come to God. God loves us before we ever love God. God is with us! So Paul begins his challenge to the Christian community in Rome with a reference to God's mercy.

Then he speaks to them about Christian spirituality. He calls it offering themselves as a living sacrifice. This is but another way to talk about loving Jesus and loving the way Jesus loved. To love in this way would be to offer our very selves as living sacrifices. Notice the contrast with the tradition of burnt offerings. For Paul, living the Christian life meant making the best possible offering to God—one's very life. This is what we are talking about when we speak of Christian spirituality. Anyone who takes Christian spirituality seriously is making a commitment to pick up the cross of unconditional love, which is the ultimate sacrifice a Christian can make.

What follows next is the reason Paul believes Christians should want to do this. It is in order to live a life that is "well-pleasing" to God. Some translators use the words "holy and acceptable." Such a translation is far too tame for what Paul is talking about. The word translated "acceptable" can also be translated "well-pleasing," which better fits Paul's urging that Christians offer ourselves as living sacrifices, living a holy life, going through a metamorphosis or transformation. Living in a way that is acceptable to God hardly suggests holiness, and certainly does not fit the image of sacrifice. Receiving a grade of "C" may be acceptable, but it is hardly much of a sacrifice for a student to achieve this level of work. Only a minimum of work is required for an "acceptable" grade of "C." But work that is "well-pleasing" gets a "B," or even an "A." This is work that requires sacrifice, that demands the best of a student. Paul apparently believed that this was the kind of offering of ourselves God expects of Christians. We are to live a life that pleases God, not a life that simply gives to God only the bare minimum. In fact, the apostle says it is "reasonable" for God to expect this kind of response to Jesus. The phrase "spiritual worship" at the end of Romans 12:1 may fit the notion of symbolic sacrifice rather than literal, but it misses the mark in terms of pleasing God. A more appropriate way to translate this phrase is "reasonable worship," which suggests that offering ourselves as a living sacrifice that pleases God is something that is reasonable. That is, it is not unreasonable that we are asked to give all we are to God in light of God's giving us so much in Jesus Christ.

To reach a level of commitment that begins to take discipline seriously in the spiritual life is to want to live a life that pleases God, that is more than simply "getting by." This desire to please God in itself becomes a motivator for taking responsibility for our own spiritual maturity. But, unfortunately, the empirical evidence confirms that even this is seldom enough to keep us going. The truth is, desire often wanes after initial enthusiasm when routine takes over. Here is where most people falter. We have good intentions. We want more than wishing for spiritual maturity. But after a period of serious discipline, the hard work of spirituality becomes evident. We find it increasingly difficult to maintain commitment to practicing spiritual disciplines, of praying on any regular basis or for any extended period of time. It is here that the issue becomes a matter of will.

The will to stay on the journey is the final step in becoming a disciplined person in regard to spiritual growth. Having the will to keep going means doing what it takes to grow, whether we feel like it or not. It means accepting without qualification or condition that we are the ones who must play a decisive role in our own spiritual maturity. We already noted the central role of the Holy Spirit, but the reality is that the Spirit cannot make us grow unless we put ourselves in the position for growth. To do this requires the will to do it. Having the will is to be disciplined, and discipline is our personal responsibility.

While the spirituality Scott Peck talks about in his popular book *The Road Less Traveled* is generic rather than specifically Christian, his candid discussion regarding people's failure to stick to much of anything that requires personal discipline is helpful. In his practice as a psychiatrist he found that the majority of people quit the hard work of becoming emotionally healthy the moment it became clear that the key to their recovery depended on the work they were willing to do. As he described it:

> As soon as patients discover that they will be required by the process of psychotherapy to assume total responsibility for their condition and its cure, most patients, no matter how eager for therapy they initially appeared to be, will drop out. (Peck, 295)

He goes on to say that the core issue in regard to the lack of discipline is, as the quote at the chapter's beginning indicates, "laziness." Further, the most frequent expression of laziness is the fear of growing up. The fear of growing up is the fear of taking responsibility for our own lives. Peck calls growing up a "fearful leap," and "it is a leap that many people never really take in their lifetime" (150). He says we resist being disturbed about ourselves, and change disturbs us. This despite the fact that change initially feels exciting. Peck is convinced that a sure mark of spiritual maturity is our awareness of just how lazy—fearful— we are. No one is exempt from the problem, but everyone can do something about it, if we choose to do so. Such a choice, he says, means letting our "healthy" self control our attitudes. The will to grow spiritually is a choice to let our "healthy" self control our lives.

This choice to work at growing spiritually is as critical to the practice of Christian spirituality as it is for other types. But being self-disciplined, having the will to work hard and persistently, needs motivation. Beyond wanting to please God, there needs to be an additional motivation for sticking to the disciplined spiritual life. I want to suggest that just such a motivation is implicit in the Romans 12 passage we have been discussing. Recall that in 12:1 Paul mentions the mercy of God.

This is more than a theological concept. I interpret Paul to be saying that the mercy of God can be trusted. This is the key. The only response one can give to such an incredible reality—that divine love can be counted on, trusted—is genuine gratitude.

Here is all the motivation Christians need in order to stay with nurturing ourselves in the life of the Spirit. If we believe in God, and being a Christian suggests that we do, since confessing Jesus as Savior and Lord means to confess God as God, then the only response that makes any sense is simple gratitude. In Jesus we are the recipients of grace. In Jesus, God reveals that we are accepted. Being grateful enough for Jesus to give to God our very best selves is a way of saying "Thank you." Indeed, how can one claim to love Jesus and not be grateful to God? Perhaps this is where church leaders are failing most the people they lead. Perhaps we are failing to help them understand that their relationship to Jesus is one way of showing genuine gratitude to God.

Is there a more complete or perfect reason than gratitude for Christians working in a disciplined way to please God? If expressing gratitude by seeking to please Jesus with our lives is not sufficient motivation for a Christian to work at spiritual nurture and growth, it is doubtful anything else will. Not that the church has not tried other things. Much of the hell fire and damnation preaching the church has done through the centuries has been an effort to get people to take God seriously. In today's churches hell fire and damnation have been replaced with more than a moderate use of guilt as a motivator among theological conservatives and liberals. Conservatives use guilt to motivate moral goodness, whereas liberals use it to promote social responsibility.

It seems that Christian leaders today believe that gratitude does not have sufficient power to tame the sinful impulses of human nature. So we try to scare people, or make them feel guilty. But Jesus did neither. Instead he preached about a loving God and invited people to serve this God who would sustain them no matter what. It seems reasonable to suggest that Jesus talked about loving God and neighbor, not out of fear or guilt, but out of gratitude. The incident of the healing of the ten lepers (Luke 17:11–19) suggests that gratitude is the appropriate response to God's initiative in our lives. Only one leper understood this, but he became the example for all the others, and for us. He was grateful for what Jesus did for him.

Gratitude—a noble and empowering motivator in the spiritual life. It is not what God will do to us if we ignore spiritual nurture and growth that will motivate us to work at them. It is what God can and will do *with* us when we do that is the real motivation Christians need. We know God will work on our behalf if we work with God because God has already reached out in love through Jesus, before we ever loved God. Taking the spiritual life seriously is our great thanksgiving for what God has done. Getting into heaven, though that would be desirable, cannot motivate us to live a life that pleases God. Avoiding the pit of hell, though that too would be desirable, cannot do it either. Pleasing God is rooted in simple gratitude. Gratitude moves us from wanting, to having, an iron will to please God.

But there is more. Once we have the motivation for staying on the journey, there are some more practical things we can do to help ourselves. I want to suggest three that have proven helpful.

The first is to find someone with whom we agree to be accountable for the commitment we make to a disciplined spiritual life. The Church of the Savior in Washington, D.C., has found this to be an effective tool. Accountability creates a relationship with another person or persons wherein we are loved, supported, and expected to fulfill the commitments we have made. Such a relationship means we are not left to ourselves alone to become disciplined. Being accountable to another person has proven to be of immense value to people in various areas of life. Employers use time clock cards to keep employees accountable for work hours. Weight Watchers weighs participants at weekly meetings. Exercise clubs offer methods of keeping people disciplined. My wife and I joined a fitness center where a record was kept of the days we were there and what exercises we did. The manager would sometimes walk through the workout with us to keep us on track.

Accountability also helps when we want to be disciplined in our spiritual life. A simple and practical way is to team up with someone who will not let us off the hook. It can become a partnership in which two people help each other to stay on the journey, and to get going again when we have stopped along the way.

The second suggestion is to accept the fact of inconsistency, especially for the beginner. It is easy to quit the struggle to be disciplined simply because of a reccurring inconsistency in working with spiritual disciplines. The way to deal with this is to accept inconsistency as a fact of life. No one is perfectly disciplined, nor does anyone need to be. Inconsistency is a problem only when we allow it to be. The thing to do about inconsistency is to keep working to overcome it. Accepting the problem of inconsistency is how we make it less of a problem. It is really that simple. The only real failure in Christian spirituality is giving up. I know of no one who does not experience inconsistency when it comes to spiritual growth. The reason is rather obvious. All of us are human. We don't do anything perfectly, including loving Jesus or loving the way he loved. Before any of us became a Christian, we were first human beings. Being a Christian does not change this reality. Even having an iron will to please God with our lives will not eliminate inconsistency in working at it. That would be the equivalent of "never making a typingg eerror!" It simply cannot be done. To try is to strive for what Emerson once called a "foolish consistency," which he went on to say, "is the hobgoblin of little minds, adored by little statesmen and philosophers and divines" (Emerson, 39).

My experience has been that accepting the reality of inconsistency in the spiritual life is a serious problem for all of us, but especially for beginners. Some may use inconsistency as an excuse for quitting the disciplined life, but most let themselves become too discouraged. They consider themselves a failure at prayer. Their humanness creates guilt (see chapter 6). This is where accountability to others can be of help. They can encourage us to accept our imperfections and challenge us to get back on the journey, for they know that success is nothing other than not giving up.

Various means of accountability are used by people committed to it. For groups, part of the meeting time can be devoted to members talking about how disciplined they have been in working at spiritual growth during the last week. One thing members often discover when this is done is that they are not alone in struggling with discipline. They also receive suggestions from one another that often prove quite helpful.

Another form of accountability is a written report to a spiritual director or a friend who has agreed to hold us accountable for being disciplined. I use this practice with my students. It provides them with an opportunity to write briefly about how they are doing, points of struggle, moments of success, and anything else they want to share. The person receiving the report may write comments on it and then return it. Such comments are to be suggestions rather than directions, as well as offering words of encouragement.

Some groups divide into pairs for the purpose of accountability. This helps the person reluctant to speak in a larger group or hesitant to write a report. An added benefit to this method is that it usually builds a special bond between the two people that can be a source of enormous strength and joy.

The point of mentioning all of these methods is to underscore the fact that accountability is an indispensable tool of discipline that helps people do the hard work that cannot be avoided when we are serious about spiritual growth and nurture.

A final suggestion is to accept that a change in daily or weekly schedules may result in an interruption of our disciplined prayer life. This is not a problem of inconsistency. It is the reality of the impact a change in schedule, especially when it involves travel, has on discipline. Changes in schedule often throw me off the track. Work-related travel, holidays, and vacations can make keeping a regular schedule very difficult. Over the years I have come to peace with myself about this. I have found that on these occasions when I tend to neglect spiritual disciplines, I get back on track once I am back on a regular schedule. This confirms my commitment to a disciplined approach to spiritual growth and nurture.

These, then, are some practical ways to help us remain faithful in working at spiritual growth and nurture. But, as we have said, in the final analysis no one or nothing can make a person disciplined. That comes from deep within, from that place in one's spirit where there burns a desire to please God in thanksgiving for the gift of Jesus Christ.

5

WAYS OF PRAYING

*Prayer is the deliberate and persevering
action of the soul.*

Julian of Norwich

Praying is basic to Christian spirituality. If communication is important in relationships, then praying is one of the primary ways Christians nurture their relationship to Jesus. Praying is talking. It is listening. It is loving. It is being loved. It is practicing the presence of the One who is the object of our devotion. It is experiencing being the object of divine love. It is all of this and more.

There are many ways to pray. Prayers have many forms and meet both common and distinctive needs. There are several forms of praying that can enrich and deepen our relationship to Jesus and to others. Those discussed here do not exhaust the possibilities but are types of prayers I have found particularly helpful because of their unique features and specific functions.

A personal word, however, is necessary before moving to this discussion, more a confession than anything else. For many years I have struggled with whether to pray to Jesus or to pray to God. Some people are surprised to discover that this is an issue. The reasons are not pertinent here. It would require a detailed discussion of the Trinity to explain. What matters is to inform you as the reader that I have been praying to both for some time now, which accounts for the fact that I refer to praying to Jesus and to praying to God throughout this discussion. The distinction between the two has blurred in my prayer life. Thus, praying to the one is praying to the other. I trust that this will not be an obstacle for you, especially since the various forms of prayer we shall discuss stand apart from the issue of to whom Christians pray.

The first form of prayer important to spiritual growth and nurture is *petitionary* prayer. We could use the term *intercessory* for this way of praying, but intercessory prayer is most often understood as one person interceding on behalf of another. Petitionary, on the other hand, is broader in scope, encompassing both intercession for others and personal prayer. For this reason this is the term we are using here.

Petitionary prayer is both underused and misused. Some people do not practice it because they don't believe in a God who must be persuaded or even asked to do something, especially since God is supposed to know everything anyway. Anthony de Mello, who was a Jesuit priest from India, challenges such thinking, arguing that how humans can change God's mind is not the issue. He says the real issue with petitionary prayer is the fact that Jesus told us to pray this way. De Mello asserts that "...petition was the only form of prayer that Jesus taught his disciples" (de Mello, 73). Further, he says that it is through petitionary praying that we learn the meaning of dependence on and trust in God. For de Mello petition is rooted in the fact that religion is "not something we 'do,' not even something we do for God. Religion is what God does for us and in us and through us..." (75). Thus, "we ceaselessly ask God for everything" to keep us aware of how much we utterly depend on God (75).

At the same time, it is always possible to misuse petitionary prayer. The image of God as a "cosmic" Santa Claus comes close to the way some people think about God. Thus, they pray as if God exists to give them what they want or think they need. Their petitions never rise above the trivial. Worse, this kind of thinking sometimes leads people to pray as if God runs a heavenly 911 rescue service available twenty-four hours a day. De Mello, of course, is calling us to a healthier and more biblical understanding of petitionary prayer through which we confess not only our need for God, but our trust in God's care and wisdom.

I am often asked how we know what to ask God for in petitionary prayer. My response is to let our desire both to love Jesus and to love the way he loved be our guide. That is another way of saying that we seek in all things to know and follow the will of God as we can discern it, and to trust that even in those instances when the divine will is unclear, we trust it is at work nonetheless. When love guides petitions, we can be confident they will not be inappropriate.

In my personal work with petitionary prayer, especially when making intercession on behalf of others, I have learned to do what I call "praying beyond my theology." This simply means that I do not allow rationality to determine the boundaries of my petitions. For example, I pray for a safe journey each time a member of my family travels. Whenever I fly I find myself praying for the plane to get off the ground. In neither instance am I sure God is involved, but I pray anyway. When it comes to more serious matters, I offer petitions and make intercession without limits. These prayers always conclude with a request for strength to face whatever must be faced, but the boundaries of the petitions are far-reaching.

It is surprising to discover how many Christians do not ask Jesus for anything specific in their praying, even though he explicitly invited us to ask, to seek, and to knock (Matthew 7:7–11; John 15:7). Ministers may be the ones who struggle more than most with the appropriateness of intercessory or petitionary prayer. I remember a pastoral care class I was in during seminary where one of the students shared an experience of being asked by a woman who had been diagnosed with terminal cancer to pray for her healing (a form of prayer we shall also discuss). Believing such a petition was in vain, he chose to pray in a way that diplomatically avoided it. Our instructor, a pioneer in the field of pastoral care and counseling, simply asked the student a question that remains vivid in my mind to this day: "Why did you give up to the doctors?"

This student had allowed his theology to view this woman's request as inappropriate, thus limiting his own capacity to make intercession for the woman. There is such a thing as selfish and self-centered petitions, often expressed to God as demands. They contradict the spirit of this form of praying and do not do justice to the appropriateness of intercessory prayer. But even when appropriate, petitions can and do run against one's theological grain. While theology certainly informs the way we respond to and participate in petitionary prayer, it need not control it. Petitionary prayer takes us into the very mystery of God, sometimes challenging us to go beyond theological concerns and boundaries.

A helpful approach to petitionary prayer is to maintain a written list of concerns and persons for whom we desire to make intercession. Each person or situation on the list is prayed for. A simple mentioning of a name or circumstance is sufficient, although extended prayer for particular persons or situations may be desirable. Sometimes I simply read through the list and then offer it up to Jesus. A small, yet helpful consequence of using a prayer list this way is learning how to pray with my eyes open. I had always prayed the traditional way of head bowed and eyes closed. I continue this practice, but now I also silently read each name or situation on the list, pausing to offer whatever petition is appropriate.

This prayer list approach may sound a bit mechanistic, but in practice it keeps us focused by eliminating the need to spend prayer time searching our memory to make sure we have not omitted a person or situation we intended to include. It also adds a sense of integrity to petitionary prayer in the fact that it helps us to keep faith with commitments we make to others to hold them in prayer. But whatever way we engage in it, petitionary prayer is an important and legitimate form of praying.

A second form of prayer is *praying scripture.* Discussions on spirituality often include instruction on what is called contemplative or sacred reading of scripture. Two traditions stand out in offering help with this: the Ignatian way (Jesuits) and the Benedictine way. They are similar, yet distinct. Ignatius described a four-step process of sacred reading (*lectio divina*): (1) walking into the scene in scripture using all five senses in order to experience the text; (2) responding to Jesus in prayer through confession, thanksgiving, and petition; (3) being present to Jesus in quiet meditation; and (4) closing with a prayer of gratitude.

Saint Benedict suggested a similar way of reading scripture contemplatively. He also described a four-step process (read, reflect, respond, rest): (1) savoring a text by reading it slowly several times and pausing to let it sink deep into us each time; (2) staying with a word or phrase that has leapt out at us, "chewing" on it in order to "taste" it fully; (3) letting a prayer be formed out of our meditation on the text, expressing feelings and thoughts; and (4) finally, resting in silence in the presence of God, waiting for some Word of the Lord to be revealed.

Each of these ways intends to let us hear scripture deep within ourselves, to make connection with it through imagination and meditation. Susan Muto has written the following reflections on contemplative reading of scripture:

> When I do spiritual reading I approach the text as a life message. I want to enter into dialogue with God's word in Holy Scripture...I hope to meet God more personally...I want the power of the word to penetrate my life. A shift has to take place from myself as master of the word to myself as servant of the word.

> What concerns us...in spiritual reading is not only what the text means in itself but what it means to me. What do those words on the page tell me about my actual situation here and now? About my relation to self, others and God? (Wells, 1982, 5-6)

While this kind of reading of scripture is desirable, and a discipline in its own right, I believe appropriating the truth and power of a scripture text as Ignatius and Benedict suggested can best be done through praying it rather than reading it. In others words, the way we can put ourselves in a text is to pray it as if the text were written to us personally. The Psalms, of course, can be, and are, used in this way. But other texts offer this possibility as well. Recently I have used this exercise in several small-group settings. Participants wrote down their prayer of scripture and shared it with the others as all of us followed in the text. It has been a marvelous experience. Several prayers and texts are listed below as illustrations of this prayer form.

+ + +

Jesus, help me to have the faith of the people who wanted to bring infants to You so You could touch them, even though they were turned away and ordered not to do it. Let me feel in my heart that You meant the words, "Let the little children come to me, and do not stop them; for it is to such as these that the kingdom of God belongs." Let me truly become as a child and learn from my children that I should receive the kingdom of God as a little child to enter fully into it. (Based on Luke 18:15–17.)

+ + +

I thank You, Lord, that in trusting in You my heart can rest and not be troubled. I believe that You are preparing a place for me and will receive me to yourself. Thank You, Jesus, for showing me that the way, the truth, and the life are knowing You. Open my heart that I may know and love You more deeply. Amen. (Based on John 14:1–6)

+ + +

Lord, you have spoken to me and proclaimed that I am your own. You have created me—you knew me before I was conceived. I give thanks that you consecrated me and appointed me even before I was formed. Lord, I often do not know the words to speak—I do not have the mind to tell. Lord, I am a child, but you, in your power, use me anyway...you have called me your servant and you have spoken through me. Let me remember that the words I speak are yours and not mine. Give me strength that I might follow your will for me, that I will always remember that you are my strength and my deliverance, that I need not fear. Thank you for touching me, for being my intimate friend, and for reaching into my life; that you have given me your words, your power, your strength, and your direction. Amen. (Based on Jeremiah 1:4-9)

+ + +

Lord, I begin by rejoicing in your name and the power of faith it represents in my life—to realize the nearness of you—a quiet word to my heart. Your presence brings a calmness and peace and well-being to my spirit. The knowledge of your power in my life—may I reach out in faith and understanding and allow that peace and power to transform me into the person you can use and allow me to greater detail Christ in me. (Based on Philippians 4:4-7)

+ + +

These examples of praying scripture reflect a freedom to express thanksgiving, praise, confession, and adoration through the words of scripture that makes it come alive for us in a personal way. Contemplative reading of scripture may do this as well, but it happens without fail when scripture is prayed.

A third form of praying is what is called *centering* prayer. This form of prayer is rich with potential. The writing of Thomas Keating, a Cistercian priest, is especially helpful in understanding centering prayer. He says the purpose of centering prayer is "to withdraw our attention from the ordinary flow of our thoughts" (Keating, 1992, 34). It is a matter of neither resisting nor entertaining these thoughts, but remaining focused on Jesus. Keating says this kind of focusing leads us to our deeper self and prepares us to engage in contemplative prayer wherein we experience union with God. Most people, he says, find themselves focused on the natural flow of thoughts when they pray. Centering prayer invites us to break from this pattern and pay attention to what lies beneath this natural flow of life. A "sacred" word or phrase is chosen to help a person clear away other thoughts. Every time a thought from the natural flow of life comes to mind, the person forms this sacred word in the mind. Christians have often employed the use of the Jesus Prayer in this way. This simple prayer says, "Lord Jesus, have mercy on me, a sinner." Centering prayer for ten or fifteen minutes a day can lead to an inner calm and peace wherein our full attention becomes focused on God (36). In this focused time the presence of God will be experienced. The result of centering prayer, Keating says, is to make a person more keenly aware of the presence of God at all times.

Keating says the primary disposition needed in the practice of centering prayer is openness to God, thus the title of the book, *Open Mind, Open Heart*. This attitude of openness is the key, and it takes no small measure of patience for one to be able to wait for the experience of God's presence (36). The combination of waiting and clearing our thoughts makes centering prayer a difficult form of praying, especially for beginners in disciplined prayer. I suspect they will find it a significant challenge. Yet it holds the potential of moving us to a deeper level in experiencing the presence of Jesus.

A fourth way of praying is *listening* prayer. On the surface this way of praying sounds like it is similar to centering prayer, but in truth it is just the opposite. In listening prayer we do sit quietly to hear what God has to say to us, but this means paying attention to thoughts rather than pushing them out through the repetition of a sacred word. Listening prayer is based upon the conviction that God speaks to us internally, that God uses human thoughts and feelings to reveal the divine will for us. The word "obedience" means "to listen." In this sense listening praying is an act of obedience, trusting that it is possible to discern the word of the Lord to us and for us, if we listen.

Listening is not easy, of course. The practice has become a lost art. Talking more than listening characterizes human relationships, so why would we be different in our relationship to Jesus? While we have already affirmed the rightful place of petitionary prayer in Christian spirituality, it becomes too much when that is the only way we pray. The word "watchful" is a helpful description of what listening prayer is all about. Being watchful is to be alert, discerning, attentive to what is going on within us. It is paying attention to the "stream of consciousness" flowing in our minds and hearts. Listening prayer may involve the practice of silence and the practice of solitude. But the focus is on listening for the purpose of discernment.

One way to practice listening prayer is to sit quietly after reading scripture or other material, paying attention to all the thoughts that come to mind, and all the feelings that arise in one's heart. The intention is to listen to one's thoughts and feelings to see what they have to teach us. Jesus speaks to us through them. A key question in listening prayer, therefore, is "What is the word of the Lord in my thoughts and feelings flowing through me?" Let me illustrate this form of praying.

I read Ecclesiastes 3:1–8. After reading the entire section, I found my mind and heart focused on 3:1: "For everything there is a season, and a time for every matter under heaven." As I pondered this verse, specific thoughts came to mind. The first was the faith that the writer must have had to believe that for everything there is a time and a season. This did not seem fatalistic to me but impressed me as an expression of profound faith in God. A second thought I had was that I was not sure I had such faith, and certainly not this kind of faith. I don't know if I believe there is a time and season for everything. The third thought I had was that if there is a time and season for everything, my problem is that most of the time I don't know what time or season it is. I pondered those thoughts for a while; then I began to pay attention to what I was feeling. The first feeling I recognized was a sense of calm as I thought about the fact that perhaps there is a time and season for everything, which means life is in hands other than my own. Immediately the calm passed and I began to feel some sense of dis-ease, anxiety even, because I'm not sure I truly believe there is a time and season for everything. I decided to pray through all these thoughts and feelings. I didn't leave them in my mind and heart. I offered them to Jesus and asked him to help me see truth in this text and to deal with the feelings the text had created in me, related to the role I play in my own life.

Listening prayer is one way we can bring thoughts and feelings together as we pray. We may listen to a scripture text, or we may listen to something else we have read, or simply seek to be present to whatever thoughts and feelings we are having at the moment to see what they have to teach us. Then we pray through them. Elaine Prevallet speaks of "listening for decisions" rather than making decisions. She writes that the Spirit gives us "nudges" to help us discern direction for our lives (Prevallet, 6). This is what it means to practice listening prayer. We trust that God will reveal the divine will in a way we can understand if we will be still and listen for it.

As spiritually rich as listening prayer can be, it has the capacity also to be disturbing. One reason for this is that it tends to reveal just how much "inner noise" we have. External "voices" get internalized. When we sit quietly to listen prayerfully to what God is saying to us, we often become embroiled in the "noise" inside us that the external world has put there. We do not always realize the degree to which "inner noise" dominates us. Moreover, it is no easy task to discern the voice of God from all the other "voices" that are inside us. Thus, the counsel of others, whether through books, the reading of scripture, or conversations, and the lessons learned from personal experience, all play a role in this discernment.

Listening prayer may reveal the depth of our personal pain and struggle. It may force us to confront situations we have tried to avoid or ignore. God works in this kind of prayer to bring us to reality. In this

way listening prayer stretches us in uncomfortable ways. It is not easy to
listen to what we have been avoiding. What is easy is to stop praying.
But this is not the way to go deeper in our capacity to love and to grow
in the ways we have discussed. If we stay with listening prayer in the
face of being stretched in uncomfortable ways, we eventually reach a
new place where we sense an inner calm that transcends all the "noise"
inside. Here we encounter the love of God in Jesus that is the basis for
our loving him and loving the way he loved.

Closely related to listening prayer is another form of praying. It is
praying through journaling. Below are some examples of this form of
prayer. They were written by different people, using different forms.
Two of them are actual prayers. Two of them are flowing thoughts that
have the spirit of prayer. All of them are poignant examples of praying
through journaling.

+ + +

You'd think I'd learn, Lord, that I can't change the world!
But I keep trying! Or at least wishing that
in many and varied ways
things were somehow different than they are.

So I set out to change
my family, my parishioners
my friends, the unfriendly sales clerk
the distracted parking lot attendant
the Federal government, the President
the Senators from my state
the Representative of the 6th District
anyone, everyone.

No wonder I get tired!!
To change the world—even to wish to change the world—
is like thinking I can carry my car up the street!

To think that I need to be a part of everything
that happens in my sphere of influence to make sure

it happens the way I think it should happen is a
sure-fire recipe for burn-out!

What's that, Lord, you're just reminding me that
I can't change the world?
Shouldn't even waste too much energy wishing I could?
But you have a suggestion??
What's that, Lord?
Give thanks?? That's it Lord, give thanks??

Will that change the world, Lord?
It won't?
It'll change WHAT??
It'll change ME?

That's what giving thanks is all about, isn't it, Lord?
Recognizing life as a gift.
Celebrating the people around us.
Savoring moments of joy.
Appreciating things as they are.
Enjoying a good meal.
Drinking in the beauty of a sunrise.
Marveling at the complexity of the human body.
Relishing simple pleasures.
Treasuring friends and family.

What's that Lord?
If I can give thanks more and more, it'll ease my
grip on things, relax my soul, make me more accepting,
lessen the likelihood of burn-out, and generally make me
a happier person??!!

Lord, if all that happened, the world would look
different to me, wouldn't it?
And I wouldn't feel the need to change it!!

+ + +

Dear God, I am grateful for all that you have given me in the last few weeks. It has been difficult, but you have brought me through this time in the desert. Though I wandered, I am back home for a while, and I'm a little more trusting of you and of your grace.

Thank you for my spiritual director and his profound wisdom. Thank you for my A.A. sponsor and his infectious, gentle spirit and his honesty. Thank you for the churches that sponsor me, and for gifts that come unexpectedly.

Thank you, Lord for my wife. I praise you for her courage and perseverance. She is a true gift from you. I give you praise, Lord, for my daughter, and for the fact that she seems to be doing well in spite of our mistakes and inconsistencies. It is a pleasure to be able to witness the daily miracles of her growth, as she asks new questions and learns to pray and tell jokes.

I'm back home for awhile Lord, and I pray that I've learned something from being in the desert. I pray that I will do a better job of trusting you and of staying out of my own way. I pray that I can learn to sit quietly a little longer when I have doubts. I ask your forgiveness for the times I try to control others because of a lack of trust in your grace. Forgive me when I try to run the show. When I go back out into the wilderness, let me trust you a little more. And during those times when I can't have what I want, let me want what I have. Amen!

+ + +

"Reverend Jones, I need you to bless this for me and give it back to me next week," said Flora as she pressed a small object into my hand after worship. And out the door she flew. The object was a four-ounce bottle of olive oil, purchased at a local drug store. Generic brand, price tag still on it (59 cents).

On the drive home I went over my options. "Little brown jug of reconstituted plastic, filled with oil which has never known virginity, boasting a rear label reading 'FOR USE ON SALADS AND OTHER FOOD ITEMS', I bless you." Giggling ensued.

Then came the feeling of shame. Not shame because of the humor—I believe humor can have amazing therapeutic value in almost any situation. But shame because my knee-jerk reaction to Flora's request was one of levity, rather than compassion. You see, I know what Flora is going through. A black woman in her sixties (her race indicating significant courage in being the only nonwhite face to appear with regularity in worship), she endures daily abuse from her alcoholic husband and crack-addicted kids. Flora rails against it all in the name of Jesus and God. Indeed, back during the summer Flora had requested that I come and anoint her daughter Grace, who had been recently diagnosed with lupus. I complied.

Who am I to place limitations on God, in my life or anyone else's? To Flora, I am holy, I am her minister—the minister who baptized her into the Lord about a year ago.

And so this week I set aside some time apart from my regular morning devotional period. In darkness, save the flicker of my little oil lamp, I prayed. I prayed hard, "God I thank you for sending Flora into my life. I thank you for her humbling demonstration of faithfulness, and for her reminder to me that I am called into your service." And then I asked God to bless the oil that it might be used in accordance with his will, and I prayed for healing and wholeness for Grace, and for Flora's family.

+ + +

Journaling offers a tangible way to pray. During a spiritually arid time in my own life, journaling prayer was the primary way I prayed for almost two years. This was not the case before this arid period, nor has it been since, although I still pray through journaling on occasion. But there was a time when it was the only form of praying I did, and it sustained and nurtured me. At the present time it is quite common for my journaling to begin with free-flowing thoughts, only to turn into a prayer in the middle of it. It is clear to me now that everything I write is a form of praying that helps me to make connection with God.

Nouwen identifies why this kind of prayer can be so beneficial:

> What I am gradually discovering is that in the writing I come in touch with the Spirit of God within me and experience how I am led to new places. Writing is a process in which we discover what lives in us. The writing itself reveals to us what is alive in us. The deepest satisfaction of writing is precisely that it opens up new spaces within us of which we were not aware before we started to write. To write is to embark on a journey whose final destination we do not know. Thus, writing requires a real act of trust. We have to say to ourselves: "I do not yet know what I carry in my heart, but I trust that it will emerge as I write." (Durback, 28)

A sixth form of prayer is *praying through art*. Icons, paintings, architecture, and various forms of writing have long been expressions of Christian faith. Praying through art, or art as prayer, as some would phrase it, goes a step further and makes the process of creation and the moment of encounter with art forms in themselves experiences of prayer.

On the walls of our seminary hang prints of great religious art of the ages. Standing in front of one of the prints when the hallways are quiet (there actually are such times) can easily become a prayerful moment as one experiences the spirit and power of the piece. Images and colors and scenes become a prayer no less real than any prayer prayed with words. On two occasions I have had students in a spiritual formation class who were artists turn in a final paper that was composed of what they called "prayer drawings," and for the artist and the viewer they were. Paintings and drawings as prayer begin with no end in mind. The artist seeks to be led rather than to follow a preconceived plan.

Recently an artist came to this same class to discuss spirituality and art. At one point she distributed single sheets of unlined paper and pencils, turned on meditative music, and invited each of us to draw lines on the paper to represent the music as we heard it. That was it! Yet it was unmistakably clear when she turned off the music that this classroom had been transformed into a sanctuary of prayer. Music has the power to do this.

During weekend silent retreats I lead, there is always a period of two hours on Saturday afternoon when recorded music conducive to meditation and prayer is played. Retreatants may use this time as an opportunity to sit quietly in the room and let music lead them in their prayers. They have reported having some very significant moments of prayer at such times.

Once during a silent retreat, I entered the convent chapel to pray. No one else was there. After a few minutes one of the sisters came in, went to the marvelous pipe organ, and began to play. I sat for nearly an hour listening and praying. When I left I had a sense that I had been on holy ground, perhaps even in the presence of Jesus himself. I have since learned that others have had similar experiences.

For many people liturgical dance has become a prayer experience. In a church I served, a young woman's interpretation of the Lord's Prayer through dance was always a deeply prayerful experience for the congregation.

Art can touch our souls in a way that nothing else seems to. It invites us out of our left brain, whose needs are rational, verbal, logical, and linear, into right brain moments that are non-rational, non-verbal, intuitive, and holistic. Such moments may lead to word prayers. At other times words would be intrusive.

Attitude plays a significant role in praying through art. The issue is intentionality. Often we view an art piece or sit and listen to music with no thought of God or Jesus, with no conscious effort to pray. But once we consciously begin to make contact with God in these moments, the experience is transformed into prayer.

A seventh form of prayer is *praying through acts of love*. Loving acts are a nontraditional form of praying, yet it is one of the ways we can pray "without ceasing" (1 Thessalonians 5:17). As we have already noted in chapter 1, compassionate acts can be moments when the presence of Jesus becomes very real to us. Such acts begin where we are, in families, in churches, in work places, in neighborhoods. The circle soon expands to all those with whom we come into contact, especially the poor and the marginalized.

Some scholars interpret Jesus' parable of the judgment of the nations as a promise that we would experience his presence in service to others (Matthew 25:31ff). If this is true, then loving acts toward others in every relationship we have—and in loving acts to the hungry, the naked, the sick, and the imprisoned—are prayer moments because they are moments in which we encounter the presence of Jesus, and are blessed because of it.

> Ministry is, first of all, receiving God's blessing from those to whom we minister. What is this blessing? It is a glimpse of the face of God. Seeing God is what heaven is all about! We can see God in the face of Jesus, and we can see the face of Jesus in all those who need our care. (Nouwen, 1994, 83)

The final form of prayer to focus on is *healing prayer*. A form of petitionary or intercessory prayer, the renewed interest in and practice of healing prayer among churches of various denominations warrants special attention. Those who are actively engaged in healing ministry believe it is rooted in the heart of a God who is loving and desires healing for God's people. They believe the healing ministry of Jesus should be a part of his continuing ministry through the church. These people are not Oral Roberts types. They are committed church members and clergy who believe healing is an important part of the gospel. They remind all of us that Jesus offers various kinds of healing to people today, just as he did in his own earthly ministry—spiritual healing, healing of inward turmoil, social healing, and physical healing.

Each type of healing is important. Healing ministry folk also believe healing comes through many sources—skills and science, counseling, sacred rites, spiritual gifts given to the church, and the prayers of all Christians. It is this last form of healing that is our concern. This attention to healing prayer is rooted not only in the ministry of Jesus, but also in the ministry of the apostles. In Acts we are told that Peter and John encountered a lame man who was laid at the gate of the temple (3:1–10). The man asked Peter and John for money ("alms"). Peter responded, "I have no silver or gold, but what I have I give you; in the name of Jesus Christ of Nazareth, stand up and walk" (3:6). The man was healed. A colleague has observed that the church today has reversed how Peter and John responded. Instead of offering healing, we give people money. We take up offerings because we don't believe in the healing power of the gospel.

The ministry of healing prayer invites us not to give people money so much as to give them what we have—Jesus Christ as the great physician. It is what every Christian has to give. Giving money has its place, and so does healing prayer. Mark Pearson interprets healing prayer as a tangible expression of love shared within the life of the church. He believes all Christians can pray for the healing of another, because all Christians can be instruments of divine love (Pearson, 21). Yet he is careful to articulate the need for balance in terms of the various ways of healing mentioned earlier. For him healing in the church is better entitled "a ministry of wholeness" (25). He explains: "We want for ourselves and others not just to look at the specific physical, emotional or spiritual problems, but at whole lives in light of what God wants for us" (25). He also strongly affirms the need of "seeing Jesus as the source of all healing" (26).

Healing prayer has more than one form. It can be the prayer of an individual or a healing team. The praying may or may not involve anointing the person needing the healing. It can be done in private or as part of a healing service. The point is to allow the loving, healing power of Jesus to work through the loving concern of one person for another.

My personal experience with healing prayer is limited. My first experience was as a recipient. A group of colleagues in ministry who regularly practice healing prayer prayed on two occasions for some old wounds in me to be healed. In one instance I was anointed. As they prayed I felt a sense of calm and relaxation come over me. I was sitting on the floor, encircled by these friends with their hands on my head and shoulders. It was a relatively quiet experience. Some of them used what they called their "prayer language," or what in vernacular speech is called speaking in "tongues." At one point one of them asked if I was okay. Eventually my body relaxed to the point where it felt as if I could melt into the floor. Then it ended. It was a beautiful experience that began inward healing of old wounds whose effect on me I had not been completely aware of.

It was in the second experience, as I named the wounds, that healing finally came. During this experience, with only two of the members of the group that had previously prayed for me, I was asked to imagine Jesus in the scene where the hurt had occurred. When asked what Jesus was saying to me, I did not respond. I did not hear him say anything. Finally I saw him stand in front of me, reach and embrace me, and say, "It's okay." This was a more emotional time for me, but in the end my entire body relaxed as it had in the first experience. The fear and anxiety I had going into these moments dissipated during the praying. I emerged with a sense of relief that always accompanies "having done" with something one needs to have done with. I was, in fact, okay.

The experience of healing prayer where I became its instrument occurred on a weekend silent retreat. A student who had been doing some important and effective therapy work related to childhood sexual abuse approached me to ask if I would anoint her and pray for her healing. She had been reading the letter of James on the retreat where such anointing and praying is described (5:14), and she wanted to have that experience. I suggested we ask the entire group to lay hands on her at the evening worship. She agreed.

That night we gathered for worship. I shared this young woman's request with the group and invited them to be a part of it. I had taken some water from the baptismal font in the retreat center chapel. The group encircled her, and I made the sign of the cross on her forehead with the baptismal water and said, "Remember your baptism." She then knelt down, everyone placed a hand on her, and I prayed for her healing. In that moment something special happened. Others began to offer prayers for her. Then we stood in silence around her. A few knelt beside her. Some hugged each other. Before it was over, two others asked for healing prayer, with a similar experience taking place.

This experience had a profound impact on that group's life. Years later those who were present, and especially this young woman, remember that night as a healing moment.

These were experiences of emotional healing, but there is no reason to believe that this is the only kind of healing Jesus does today. Indeed, if we believe that Jesus can heal emotional wounds and pains and illnesses, why would we place limits on his power to heal in other ways? As previously noted, Mark Pearson identifies science, i.e., modern medicine, as part of the healing God works through today. The point of healing prayer is to say that healing is not limited to what human beings know and can do. All forms of healing prayer have in common trust in the healing presence of Jesus. Healing is not the only way Jesus manifests himself, and not the only way healing comes to a person, as those involved in healing ministries themselves emphasize. But this form of praying is one about which Christians today need to become more informed in order to be open to its potential power.

Praying, then, takes many forms. Each of us must find our comfort level in practicing them. But all of these forms witness to faith in the living reality of the presence of Jesus Christ in the lives of Christians today. Thus, each one has the potential for nurturing our capacity to love Jesus and to love the way Jesus loved.

6

THE STRUGGLE WITH DISCOURAGEMENT

I do not understand my own actions. For I do not do what I want, but I do the very thing I hate.

The apostle Paul (Romans 7:15)

A simple reality we need to keep in mind as we work at spiritual growth and nurture is that even though we are Christian, we never stop being human. This means that the work does not grow easier with the passage of time. While we are blessed with many strengths, at the same time being human means we never cease contending with the weaknesses, frailties, and outright sins that go with being human. Certain realities are endemic to being human and, therefore, confront the purest of souls with obstacles that make the path to spiritual maturity difficult. This fact of life has the potential of causing us to give up on ourselves and even God. We can easily become discouraged about the work spirituality involves, and the growth it is supposed to bring but doesn't seem to. In light of this, I want to discuss some of the manifestations of "the human condition" that seem to press themselves upon us more than others. Loving Jesus and loving the way he loved, moving from one level of spiritual maturity to another—all of this is work enough. Discouragement can kill our spirits if we are not prepared for the impact our humanness has on us as Christians.

The first of these is the very thing with which honest Christians constantly struggle, but which must be present in order for Christian spirituality to have any meaning at all—faith itself. It is easy to underestimate both the significance and difficulty of being a person of faith. In this age of skepticism and cynicism, faith itself is a bold act. Human confidence in science and technology as the primary and at times sole means of solving problems runs deep and wide in modern culture. Christians have a different view of reality. We see problems from the perspective of character. We believe sin is real and must be factored into the equation of every situation. Further, we are convinced that science and technology ignore the reality of sin to the peril of civilization itself. The mere existence of nuclear weapons that can destroy the earth as we know it, for example, leaves little doubt in the mind of any reasonable person that human ingenuity alone cannot save us. But it can destroy us, and that is the danger Christians do not want to ignore.

For Christians morality goes to the core of decision making. We clearly have the power to destroy the planet through nuclear holocaust or environmental destruction, and to wreak havoc on a lesser scale daily, but from the Christian perspective humans do not have the authority to do so. That authority, we believe, belongs to God. This is the witness of faith the world needs, whether it knows it or not.

Yet the world we live in is not one that encourages faith in anything beyond human ability. The challenge to people of faith is to witness to the hope of faith in spite of the world's lack of it. This is precisely what the writer of 1 John understood when he wrote:

> For the love of God is this, that we obey his commandments. And his commandments are not burdensome, for whatever is born of God conquers the world. And this is the victory that conquers the world, our faith. Who is it that conquers the world but the one who believes that Jesus is the Son of God? (1 John 5:3–5)

It is not surprising that the world does not recognize the significance of faith. What is surprising, however, is the fact that many Christians don't either. Churches are full of members who do not understand the power of the witness of faith itself. Most of the energies of Christians are focused on living the truth that we are to be "doers of the word, and not merely hearers" (James 1:22). And rightly so. But 1 John reminds us that faith itself is also an important witness to the truth we believe in and the truth the world needs if it is to survive.

Perhaps we overlook the significance of faith because it is difficult to make it a defining reality for our lives. Most Christians acknowledge that doubt is part of being a believer. Yet doubts are troublesome for us, especially when we confront so much innocent suffering. When the federal building in Oklahoma was bombed, the senselessness of innocent suffering, especially the children, shook the foundations of people of faith everywhere. The same thing happened with the news of Susan Smith's drowning of her own two little boys in South Carolina. How does one believe in a good God in the face of things like this? Most of us ultimately don't throw in the towel and turn cynical. But it is a struggle not to. Holding on to faith is not something to be taken for granted.

I think Jesus anticipated the difficulty of being a person of faith when he told Thomas: "Have you believed because you have seen me? Blessed are those who have not seen and yet have come to believe" (John 20:29). If we could see and touch and listen to Jesus in person, the difficulties of faith might not be so difficult to cope with. But we do not have this opportunity. Faith is our only option. It is far more bold to choose to be a person of faith than not to be. The easy way out is agnosticism. It takes courage to dare to believe without the benefit of widespread empirical evidence to support us.

The fact that there is a mystical dimension to Christian faith does not make the spiritual journey any easier. How do we develop a relationship with someone who is not present in the flesh? Here again, Jesus' words to Thomas describe our situation. We are the ones who must believe without seeing, and that immediately confronts us with the reality of mystery. If there were no innocent suffering to disturb us, it would remain a challenge to make sense of Christian claims about reality anyway, simply because of the nature of our faith. We are people who speak of experiential truth. Many Christians have tried and continue to try to make Christianity into a propositional faith. That is, they define being a Christian in terms of believing certain things. Others define it as doing certain things. Still others define it as believing and doing. While each of these contains an element of truth, all of them go back to the story of the experience of the first disciples being encountered by Jesus, who was raised from the dead, a story whose truth has been experienced by others up to the present.

This story is an outrageous claim that does not have universal acceptance even among Christians. Why? Because such faith is difficult for us. It requires an acceptance of the reality of mystery, not simply that which is unknown, but what is, in the truest sense, unknowable. This kind of faith rejects the temptation to limit what is real to scientific understanding or natural laws. The core of Christian spirituality is, as we have said, that we can believe in and also know Jesus, love him, and experience the reality of his resurrection for ourselves.

Christian spirituality is difficult precisely because it requires faith. It is unlikely that a nonbeliever can be led to believe through the practice of spiritual disciplines. A person who does not have a foundation of faith upon which to build a relationship with Jesus will not invest the necessary time and energy that spiritual growth requires. Practicing disciplines make no sense apart from the presence of faith. Contemplative prayer seems to be a futile, if not bizarre, exercise in superstition and hocus pocus.

The difficulty faith presents may not seem to be a real issue for us. Perhaps faith is a problem for people new to the church, or people who are prone to questions and doubts, but not to anyone who has been around the church for a long time. Such an attitude, however, reveals a lack of awareness of what Saint John of the Cross in the sixteenth century called the "dark night of the soul." This is the sense of spiritual barrenness many devout Christians experience, where God seems far off and one is left to one's own wits to survive. This is an experience people of faith have. It is, in fact, faith that produces it. John of the Cross went so far as to suggest that God created the "dark nights of the soul" to humble Christians. Whatever the cause, there are periods in the lives of believers that "feel" as if we have been abandoned by the God we believe in. But that "feeling" is itself an expression of faith. Without faith there would be no experience of God's presence and absence. Life would be completely in the hands of chance. It is only because of faith that Christian spirituality makes any difference to us at all.

A second difficulty stems from the fact previously mentioned that Christians are people who take sin seriously. We do so because of personal experience with it. We are people who understand the words of the apostle Paul noted at the beginning of the chapter:

> I do not understand my own actions. For I do not do what I want, but I do the very thing I hate....I do not do the good I want, but the evil I do not want is what I do. Now if I do what I do not want, it is no longer I that do it, but sin that dwells within me. (Romans 7:15, 19–20)

Within most of us is the haunting suspicion that the concept of original sin, first articulated by Saint Augustine and later de facto adopted by the church as doctrine, accurately depicts the human condition. We may believe creation began, as Matthew Fox argues, in "original blessing" rather than original sin. Yet we cannot escape the fact that we continue to sin, even when we have an earnest desire not to.

The effect of the unrelenting nature of sin in regard to Christian spirituality is discouragement. Try as we may, we seem to fail more than succeed in loving Jesus and loving the way he loved. There are moments when we experience what we believe is a holy presence in our lives, while other moments are filled with a sense of void. This is the crucible within which Christians live. It is easy to be overwhelmed with a sense of futility when we are honestly self-reflective and see ourselves for what we are and what we do. The best of people fail miserably to live up to the best that is within them. The rest of us seem to do worse than that.

It is ironic that Christians would be so troubled about the reality of sin. Not that we should not be grieved by our actions, especially when they hurt others. But the gospel is candid about sin. Indeed, scripture is one body of literature that challenges naive trust in human ability precisely because biblical writers take sin so seriously. The fact that Christians are surprised and troubled by sin, especially when it shows its ugly head in the church, suggests that we have been unduly influenced by utopian optimism rooted in science and technology. That people are selfish, greedy, and mean-spirited should come as no news to Christians. Realism is one way we can help ourselves cope with the inevitable. This is not to suggest that the ubiquitous nature of sin should lull us into complacency about it or lead to a flippant attitude about its effect. It is only to say that sin is a fact of life. The work of Christian spirituality begins with the assumption and functions in spite of it.

Some of the discouragement related to frustration with the reality of sin is rooted in the tendency to measure spiritual progress at every turn. We have already noted this danger in chapter 2. Taking seriously sin's power to discourage is important precisely because it is easy not to. Indeed, Christians tend to think assessment of our spiritual life is not only a good idea but is encouraged in scripture by such statements as the apostle Paul's words in Romans 12:3: "For by the grace given to me I say to everyone among you not to think of yourself more highly than you ought to think, but to think with sober judgment, each according to the measure of faith that God has assigned." This is good advice if we understand and believe we live and move and have our very being because of divine grace. Otherwise, assessment leads to discouragement as we buckle under the weight of our own sin.

We can help ourselves deal with discouragement by understanding that spiritual growth is more circular than linear. It does not run in a straight line. It is more a matter of going "around and around" with our weaknesses and sins. My journal of twenty-five years reveals a constant struggle today with many of the issues I confronted when I first began to journal. This could be interpreted as making no progress, of being a sign of little spiritual growth. Or it can be understood as the nature of spiritual development, which is more like taking small steps forward and backward than of simply making giant leaps forward. This is why we previously described spiritual growth as movements. Until we understand and accept that this is the nature of spiritual growth, we will continue to be discouraged about it.

Another factor that makes us susceptible to discouragement is the lack of spiritual nurture from the church. We made reference to this in chapter 1 and will suggest some things the church can do about it in chapter 7. But we also must be clear about the influence the state of the church today has on personal spiritual growth. More than a few Christians who want to grow spiritually find participation in church life a hindrance rather than a support in their journey. To see how much the church is run like a business, to hear the way Christians talk to and about one another, to see or feel the discouragement of clergy, can take the wind out of the strongest of "spiritual" sails. Recently a minister friend who is four years from retirement said that he would retire today if he were in a financial position to do it. This man has served in his current pastorate for over twenty years. He is committed and competent and recognized by colleagues as one of the best. But his spirit is low. He says the conflicts he has confronted in the church have made prayer more necessary and at the same time more difficult. His experience is commonplace today.

The church is quite often the last place that nurtures and encourages people who take spirituality seriously. The situation is not hopeless, but it is real, and those of us who work at spiritual growth cannot ignore or escape it. The human condition with which we contend individually also infects our collective life in the church. Moreover, the power of corporate sin, as theologian Reinhold Niebuhr pointed out years ago, far exceeds individual sin (Niebuhr, 1932). This is as true in the church as it is in secular society. Naivete about this can cause even the most devout Christian to lose heart.

Our point is this: because discouragement is a deterrent to discipline in the spiritual life, accepting the fact that the realities of the human condition are always at work in us minimizes the potential for prolonged discouragement. Being Christian and being human at the same time is the only choice we have, if we choose to follow Jesus.

7

MARKS OF A
SPIRITUALLY
MATURE CHURCH

To fight for integrity of membership within existing structures is certainly extraordinarily difficult, but there is hardly any path that frees one from that struggle.

Elizabeth O'Connor

Loren Mead, founder of the Alban Institute, has written: "Everyone I know who works in the church knows there is trouble. Churches just don't 'work' the way they used to" (Mead, 1994, vi). His assessment is probably accurate on both counts. Leaders in the church know there is trouble in the church, and churches *don't* work the way they used to. There may not be agreement on why there is trouble and why churches don't work the way they used to, but there is general agreement that both propositions describe the situation in the church as it really is.

A colleague recently used the image of an earthquake to describe what is happening in the church. He was intentionally contrasting the frequently used image of the church being pummeled by rough winds on a stormy sea, but settling down when the storm has passed. In an earthquake the tectonic plates under the earth that provide a foundation upon which we stand shift ever so slightly, but in that shifting nothing is ever the same. This, he believes, describes the church's situation today. The foundations have been shaken, and the future will reflect the reality that everything has changed.

That is not all bad. Current problems may indicate that the church of today is in a kind of wilderness that is part of the journey to a new land. The Christian community may be experiencing the birth pangs of a new life. What the church will look like in the future is anybody's guess, but there is a chorus of believers such as Mead who see a new church being born (see Mead's *The Once and Future Church*).

One thing is clear, however. "Business as usual" in the church is not a viable option. The spiritual aridity people feel today in their personal lives has also enveloped most churches. The real problem facing churches is not numerical or financial decline. These are symptoms. The real problem is spiritual. Churches are trying to live without any serious connectedness to Jesus, who is the source of the church's life. We have gone after all the programs, strategies, and techniques anybody has come up with in search of new life. But none has quenched our thirst because none is the source of living water. Confronting the church's spiritual aridity is the primary issue today. What is more, the nature of this problem does not lend itself to a quick fix. People do not grow up spiritually overnight. Roots take time to go down deep. Without patience in attending to spiritual roots, most of what the church tries to do to renew its life will be a cut-flower effort, blooming for a while and then withering for lack of nourishment.

For emphasis, let me say again that what we are talking about in this chapter is a collective spirituality expressed in and through the life of the "body" of Christ. The key is understanding that spirituality in the church is more than the sum of its parts. It is more than the combination of individuals who may be deeply spiritual. The church as a "body" has a spiritual life and must be attended to if the church is to understand and embody its identity and mission. The call to love Jesus and love the way he loved should not be left solely to individual response. It needs to shape and influence the way we live and move and have our being as the church.

This means churches today must attend to a reunion with Jesus Christ in their life as communities of faith. It is within the context of the church's connectedness to Jesus—that is, its collective spirituality— that it knows who it is and what it is to do. The church doesn't simply encourage spirituality. It exists for it. It witnesses to it. The church lives by means of its connectedness to Jesus, believing in him, loving him, putting him first in its life.

It is tempting to try to identify steps churches can take to do the work necessary for spiritual growth and nurture. I believe what may be more helpful, though, is to identify marks of mature spirituality in the church, similar to the signs of individual spiritual growth discussed in chapter 2. These marks serve to help churches monitor their spiritual growth and development. While the list included may not be exhaustive, at least we can point out some of the most obvious ones.

One is *worship*. This is the place where the healthiness of a congregation's spiritual life finds public expression. Worship is not tangential to the church's life. It is central. I believe the quality of a congregation's worship life reveals the quality of its life in all other aspects. A church without a vital and alive worshiping center is a church without the power of the Holy Spirit. One of the gifts the monastic tradition has given to the whole church is the sample of community life that revolves around worship. The daily schedule of worship in convents and monasteries is not realistic for congregations, but churches can learn from them that the life of any Christian community depends on worship as its center.

The fact that this is so obvious makes one wonder why ministers and church members alike take it for granted. The common complaint among mainline church members today is that worship is boring. It would be easy to dismiss such criticism as symptomatic of people's desire to be entertained, to make the sanctuary a stage and the minister a performer. But that is too facile. The truth is that much of the church's worship today is boring, not because it fails to be entertaining, but because it is not rooted in a collective spirituality that is life-giving to worship.

Nurturing worship that has the power to sustain a congregation has a variety of forms. The church year offers marvelous opportunities for rich and varied worship experiences. The key is to experience worship that invites the best of a people's praise and thanksgiving in response to the Lordship of Jesus Christ. Worship is an expression of gratitude by a faithful people. It is not a spectator sport, but an opportunity to participate in a sacred act of honoring the source of life. Highly liturgical and free church traditions alike can experience vital worship. All it takes is the right attitude, a desire to please God and not ourselves, and a people who are excited about their life and ministry together.

One of the communities of faith that is modeling creative worship that meets the needs of Christians today, but is rooted in the tradition of the church, is the Roman Catholic Church. Not all parishes are doing this, but many are, and especially on college campuses through Newman Centers. These worship experiences are vital, enriching, and spiritually nurturing through the creative blending of traditional liturgy and contemporary music. It is worship that illustrates the potential worship holds in nurturing a faith community's connectedness to Jesus Christ.

A second mark of a spiritually mature church is *members knowing their faith story.* Spiritual maturity in a congregation means members know who they are as Christians. The story of faith has the power to nurture that identity. It is a story that begins in scripture. Here is the essential resource for strengthening a congregation's commitment to loving Jesus and loving the way he loved. The New Testament connects Christians to Jesus. The Old Testament provides the context for the New Testament story. Both help Christians to know who they are and what they are to do. No other book stands equal to scripture in this regard. The Bible is the church's book. In spiritually mature congregations the Bible is preached and taught with all the passion appropriate to its primary role as a source of inspirational nurture and prophetic challenge.

But the story does not end with scripture. Thus, spiritually mature congregations are those churches that know church tradition as well as scripture. Laity often testify to how enriched they are by study of church history that roots them deeply in a tradition they discover is dynamic rather than static. When extended to the history of their particular denomination, their faith is nurtured even more. Why? Because spirituality becomes rooted in what is specifically Christian. Generic spirituality has no roots in Christian scripture or tradition and, thus, has no power to give identity. Spiritually mature churches learn the old, old story to which scripture and tradition witness and learn to tell it well. In doing so they also fulfill the mission of perpetuating it. As Robert Wuthnow has written: "The most serious task that the churches have always faced has been the transmission of an identity to new generations...." (Wuthnow, 53). Knowing the Christian story and telling it well is a clear sign of the spiritual maturity of a church.

A third mark of spiritual maturity in a congregation is the *way they make decisions*. Earlier we talked about listening prayer as a way of listening for decisions rather than simply making them. Here is where churches would do well to listen! Decision-making in most churches is anything but listening, and anything but nurturing and expressing the life of the Spirit. Most churches follow Robert's Rules of Order rather than the Holy Spirit in making decisions. We vote up or down on issues without any intentional effort to listen for the leading of the Spirit. Such a process easily turns into "winning and losing," as if there is such a thing in the body of Christ. The church's relationship to Jesus as Savior and Lord can be and often is completely ignored as it goes about making decisions.

To take spirituality seriously in the church means abandoning this way of making decisions in favor of consensus building. Rather than Robert's Rules of Order, questions such as, "How does this decision contribute to and express our commitment to loving Jesus and loving the way he loved?" and "Is there sufficient leading of the Lord for us to take this step?" become the guides for decision making. While consensus building is slower and often harder than majority rule, it reflects an attempt to let the spiritual life of church members lead them in the decisions they make.

A church in our community was led by its pastor to use this process when they faced a decision about staying in their present location or moving. His personal spiritual life was deep enough that he knew simply asking whether or nor the members wanted to move was the wrong question. Instead, he invited the church to start asking what they discerned to be the leading of the Spirit regarding what to do. He asked them to begin "listening" for the decision. During this time several acres of prime property unexpectedly became available for purchase for a good price. The church prayed and discussed whether to buy it. Their discernment of the circumstances led them to buy the land, but to do so with the conscious decision not to commit themselves to moving. It was stated publicly that there still was not sufficient clearness about that decision, and they were still waiting to know what to do. Two years later one of the women of the church said in a prayer meeting that she believed she might have a word from the Lord for the church about what to do. During her prayer time she read Deuteronomy 28:1–3 where the people are told that if they keep the commandments, blessings will come to them, with the concluding verse saying: "Blessed shall you be in the city, and blessed shall you be in the field" (28:3). Her interpretation was that perhaps Jesus was leading them not to move to the suburbs, but to plant a new congregation there. The church prayed about the "word" she thought she was hearing. They again discerned that this was the leading of the Spirit. About a hundred people felt led to make the move. The finance ministry of the church later came back to the congregation and said they sensed the Lord was leading them to suggest that the church simply deed the property over to the new congregation. The church agreed. It was done.

The minister believes that had they simply voted up or down whether or not to move, and let the majority carry the day, the congregation would have suffered a nasty split. Instead today there are two healthy, very different congregations meeting the needs of very different communities. This is what can happen when spirituality leads the church as a body to "listen" for a consensus decision rather than simply making decisions by majority rule. Churches have trouble trusting consensus building. Christians are just as impatient as anyone. We want to get things done quickly. Moreover, we can be as skeptical of the leading of the Holy Spirit in decision making as groups outside the church. It takes a commitment to draw upon the collective spirituality of a church for a congregation to have the courage and wisdom to take the time to build consensus.

A fourth mark of spiritual maturity is the way churches *nurture every member to follow a call into some form of ministry*. The ministry of all believers is a core value of the church. While the practice of setting aside particular men and women for ordained ministry is important, the ministry of the laity remains central to the life and work of all vital congregations. Churches of mature spirituality take seriously the nurturing of their members in identifying and following their specific call to some area of ministry.

The New Testament epistles are quite specific in defining the nature of the church's ministry in terms of the evoking and exercising of the gifts of the Holy Spirit (1 Corinthians 12; Ephesians 4:1–16). I suggest that spiritually mature churches are committed to living out this understanding of church life. They are unwilling to tolerate spectatorship in their membership. What is more, these kinds of churches identify the role of the ordained clergy as helping church members discern their call to a particular ministry, whether it be within the life of the congregation or outside in the community.

Unfortunately, many congregations do not have this kind of spiritual maturity. Instead, they focus on maintaining the institutional dimension of the church. They want the members to serve the church rather than the church being a vehicle through which the members serve the world. In this kind of congregation there is very little understanding of the call to ministry of the laity. For the most part, the role of the laity is to serve as members of a committee and/or a board. This service is rendered, more often than not, out of a sense of duty and obligation, which is one of the reasons committee membership is seldom a source of spiritual nurture. It is also the main reason why most of the time church committees are forced to function with only a handful of members who attend the meetings. No church would want to be led by someone ordained who was serving primarily out of a sense of obligation, yet numbers of congregations expect no better from their laity, and give no better to them.

This is not an effective way to nurture the spiritual life of a church. Ministry may cause a person to hesitate long enough to ponder the awesome responsibility they may feel called to accept, but in the end that acceptance must be done out of a sense of call rather than duty. Spiritually mature churches nurture laypeople in taking their own call to ministry seriously. They study the New Testament understanding of the church and ministry, including the usually neglected concept of the gifts of the Spirit. These churches know that the vitality of a congregation depends upon the degree to which the members are having the time of their lives doing ministry. Serving the needs of the institution alone will never create this kind of excitement. It is only when people are alive with a sense of genuine call to ministry that they become a joyful people whose faith is contagious.

One practical step in following an approach to ministry that nurtures the call of laity, a step that requires a significant degree of spiritual maturity in a church, is taking the risk of encouraging every member to exercise the freedom to say no to requests to serve until they feel like the service to be given is what God is truly calling them to do. In other words, spiritually mature churches know that a person is never free to say yes to the invitation to serve until they are free to say no. Spiritual maturity in a church means putting an end to laity serving out of a sense of obligation or "oughtness." And contrary to what one may think, when understood properly, this approach never encourages a kind of "lone ranger" mentality among the laity. On the contrary, it underscores the fact that the role of the entire community of faith is essential in helping everyone identify his or her call and get on with ministry. Discerning and following call by laity of necessity involve the wisdom, counsel, and encouragement of the whole church. Nurturing the call to ministry among the laity rests upon the conviction that the clergy are called to help call forth this ministry. Laypeople are not in the church to serve the clergy. The clergy are in the church to serve the laity. What is more, a church that chooses to function this way must have the spiritual maturity to accept the fact that the ministry of the laity is a process slow in developing and requiring a considerable degree of patience and waiting. It is not likely to produce a lot of activity in a short period of time, in part because for most churches a significant effort in reeducation about the nature of the church and its ministry will be needed. But churches that desire to express their love for Jesus in ministry will make the effort, regardless of the time or energy it takes. For in the end it is the way the church truly becomes a community for vital ministry.

Fifth, mature spirituality in churches makes itself known in the way they *deal with conflict.* Listening for decisions will contribute to fewer serious conflicts in the church, but conflicts will arise nonetheless. The quality of a congregation's spiritual life is seen in the way it thinks and acts in times of conflict. Here is where commitment to Jesus Christ as Lord is put to the test. It also is possible for prayer to guide a church through conflict, making the conflict itself a means of spiritual growth. It also is possible for conflict to occur without attention to prayer at all. It is ironic that Christians who talk at length about loving others often engage in very unloving conflict. Conflict itself is not a sign of the absence of love. It is how people deal with conflict that reveals the quality of their loving one another.

Churches that are focused in a serious way on their spiritual life will make keeping faith with the commitment to loving Jesus and loving the way he loved their primary concern. This is what matters. It is the "first thing" when conflicts occur. Not winning. Not being right. Not having our say. Not getting our way. Honoring our commitment to belonging to Jesus. This is what matters first in a church whose spiritual life is healthy. Once this is established, then a process for conflict resolution becomes possible.

Spiritually mature congregations follow specific processes for dealing with conflict that involve careful study of all sides of a controversy or conflict. The members understand that subjectivity is an inevitable part of human perception, that no one sees any issue without prejudice, and that thoughtful study is essential to any process of reconciling differences. Knowledge alone does not bring reconciliation, but reconciliation is not possible without it. It is not a cure-all, but knowledge does further understanding among spiritually mature Christians as they confront conflict.

Praying through conflict is another part of the process of reconciling differences in spiritually mature congregations. This means the people involved in conflict pray for each other while the conflict is occurring. This does not mean praying for God to open the other person's eyes to our point of view. It involves praying for the health and well-being of any person(s) with whom we are in conflict. We pray for them to have wisdom and courage. We pray for them to be able to love us in the midst of the conflict. We pray for their hurts and struggles. We pray for the presence and healing power of Jesus to be real to them. What we discover in praying for people with whom we have conflict is that it is difficult to demonize them and pray for them at the same time. Praying for them often helps us to see the plank in our own eyes when we have been focused on the speck in theirs.

Praying for people in the midst of conflict does not mean that we give up principles or compromise our integrity for the sake of harmony. It simply means we are affirming that pleasing Jesus is the focus of our lives. We know that demonizing others and self-righteous attitudes and actions do not please Jesus. This kind of praying usually leads us into asking Jesus to give us a clean heart and a right spirit as we cope with the conflict.

Praying for others often takes time. Once I shared with a trusted colleague a conflict I was having with another person. He suggested I go and talk to that person. My reply was that I still had a lot of praying to do before I was ready to do that. This is the way it is sometimes. Praying for the person with whom we are in conflict doesn't immediately resolve the issues. The effects of praying for another may take time, but if we persist in the praying we grow beyond the conflict and become committed to reconciliation.

A sixth mark of spiritually mature congregations is their *commitment to justice-seeking*. One way the church can show this commitment is the way it treats strangers. Torah law concerning the stranger in Israel, the *ger*, sheds light on why Jesus loved the way he loved. The *ger* were strangers who lived among the Jews, but did not become converts (later the term came to mean "convert"). They were to be treated with compassion and love. Torah law applied to the *ger*, not to coerce, but to remind Jews that above everything they were not to make the *ger* feel like strangers. They were not to be made to feel left out, but protected and wanted. Though strangers, they were not to be treated as strangers. They did not stand outside the community's circle of compassion, concern, and love.

Here is an example of a spiritually mature attitude embodied in a community. In a society that has reached the point of treating everyone like a stranger, and especially those without any political or economic power, the church's relationship to Jesus must surely produce the fruit of hospitality to any and all strangers. The church that knows its love for Jesus must show itself in the way it loves those who live on the margins of life, who feel forgotten and often are, who may be the cause of their own trouble, but who nonetheless need someone to love them and care for and about them.

Mother Teresa and the Missionaries of Charity serve as a compelling example of what it means to practice spirituality in the church. They talk about what the poor give them, not what they give the poor. Mother Teresa says that the first dying woman for whom she cared gave her more than she gave the woman. Mother Teresa helped the woman die with dignity. The woman helped her live with dignity. A prayer she and her sisters often pray is:

Mary, Mother of Jesus, give me your heart, so beautiful, so pure, so immaculate, so full of love and humility, that I may be able to receive Jesus in the Bread of Life, love him as you loved him, and serve him in the distressing disguise of the Poorest of the poor. (Mother Teresa, xxv-xxvi)

The church that treats the stranger, the poor, the marginalized, the lost, in the same way Jesus would treat them, indeed treats them as Jesus himself, is a church that is living close to its Lord. It is a church that truly is the Body of Christ because it is letting Jesus be its Head. It is a church that knows its reputation among the "least of these" is a pretty good measure of its faithfulness in bearing the cross to which Jesus has called it. A church in which a stranger does not feel welcomed is a church that has lost its way, and perhaps its soul.

Though not usually understood this way, I suggest that how they treat their children is also the way spiritually mature congregations express a commitment to justice-seeking. In a beautiful book of prayers on loving and working for children, Marian Wright Edelman says she started out to write a different kind of book. As founder and president of the Children's Defense Fund, she thought she might write a book on children and public policy. Instead, she said, "out tumbled prayers instead," which upon reflection she understood, writing:

As I have grown older and wearier trying to get our nation to put children first and become more worried about my own and other people's children growing up in an America where moral and common sense and family and community values are disintegrating, I pray more and more. I know that only with God's help and only with prayer...can some mountains be moved. (Edelman, xiii)

Churches may not be the only advocate for children today, but a spiritually mature church will always be a voice for them in the community in which it finds itself. The Church of the Covenant in Lynchburg, Virginia, many years ago recognized the importance of caring for children and teaching them how to appreciate diversity in color, social and economic status, religious tradition, and nationality.

In the early 1950s it began Camp Kum-Ba-Yah that intentionally brought together in the summer children from the inner city and the suburbs, black and white, to teach them these principles. Kum-Ba-Yah has for most of its existence had an international staff. In a segregated city that was shot through with racism and classism, the pastor, Beverly Cosby, became convinced that such a camp experience was one way to free children from the prejudices and injustices practiced by the larger society, and for many of them, in their own homes. Cosby and his courageous co-workers survived Molotov cocktails, accusations of communist infiltrators by the staunch segregationist editor of the newspaper, criticism, and rejection. Today in this same city, Camp Kum-Ba-Yah is recognized as a major contributor to loving children and teaching them the ways of justice-seeking, peace, and reconciliation.

This is the way any spiritually mature church will treat its children. It will love and care about them enough to show them how to love Jesus and love the way he loved by teaching them to love themselves, those around them, and the world God has created. It may be that in the end it will be the way churches treat children that will be the measure by which they are judged. For what more reveals a church's spiritual health than its actions and attitude toward children? Novelist Barbara Kingsolver says the message she is trying to give to her daughter is that from the get-go she is not just taking up space here, but is truly valuable (Kingsolver, 97). She then says: "We can see, if we care to look, that the way we treat children, all of them, not just our own, and especially those in great need—defines the shape of the world we'll wake up in tomorrow" (105). The message a spiritually mature church gives its children—all children, in fact—is that they matter, they are valuable, they are not just taking up space. That is how the church does its part in shaping the kind of tomorrow all of us will wake up in.

But justice-seeking involves more than concern for strangers and children. Because it is a matter of the head as well as the heart, justice-seeking also involves attending to systemic causes of injustice and unnecessary suffering. Taking personal responsibility for one's life is a primary focus today. It is an important corrective to an attitude among some people of blaming everyone else for problems and expecting them to take care of those problems. Yet spiritually mature congregations recognize that systems do affect people and can prolong injustices that can be ended only as the system is changed. The "isms" that are easily dismissed are in fact real and quite resistant to challenge by individual initiative alone. Congregations deeply rooted in the life of the Spirit will never be satisfied only to put Band-Aids on the wounds of people, as important as that is. These churches also are willing to challenge a status quo that ignores any prophetic word that shakes its foundations.

Recently a local minister spoke about an incident of racism on the university campus near his church that had received virtually no attention by the school paper, local media, or university officials, several of whom are members of his congregation. An African-American student had written a letter to the school paper in which she discussed racism on the campus. Two days later she was approached by two white students brandishing knives and telling her that if she didn't like her life as it was, they would be glad to end it for her. This minister's challenge to a university inclined to turn its head to a serious problem is the stuff of justice-seeking. Just as important, he is modeling for his congregation a passion for justice-seeking that he desires them to embody as a community of faith, arising from their spiritual life together.

A seventh mark of spiritually mature congregations is the capacity to love one another *through controversial issues.* We have already noted the need for clear thinking among spiritually mature Christians (chapter 2). Certainly clear-headedness plays an important role in any congregation's capacity to deal reasonably with controversy or conflict. Being able to love one another in the process goes a step further. Many congregations cope with controversial issues either by ignoring them or beating up on each other as they confront them. Both are signs of spiritual superficiality, and both are poor witnesses to the gospel. Jesus once said that the love his followers had for one another would be a primary symbol of their belonging to him (John 13:35). On this score most congregations have failed to pass the test. Instead, the pattern seems to be to allow controversial issues to divide and destroy the church's life and witness. Issues of racism and gender discrimination have pushed the church for a long time, and more often than not congregations have come up short. Now the issue of homosexuality is at the center of controversy in the church. Legitimate differences in views exist on questions related to homosexuality and the church. But what is clear is that most churches are not demonstrating the will even to discuss the issue, partly in response to the beating up on one another that has occurred in those congregations that have. I personally know of the end of one husband and wife co-pastorate, beginning the moment they initiated an educational program on the church's response to homosexual persons. In another instance, a church that sought to accept homosexuals into membership lost some seventy members almost overnight.

What difference does spirituality make if it does not inform the way we deal with one another in the church as we face controversial issues? It sometimes appears as if secular institutions are better able to deal with controversy than is the church. This hardly points to spiritual maturity in the church. Indeed, that the church is less able than non-church groups to confront controversy without acrimony is a sign of sin rather than loving Jesus or loving the way he loved. I believe the measure of any congregation's spiritual health is the degree to which its members can love each other in spite of differences in opinions and beliefs regarding controversial issues. Such congregations have the spiritual maturity to understand that the capacity to love through controversy offers a marvelous opportunity to witness to the gospel.

One last mark of spiritually mature congregations is *an overall focus on spirituality* in their life and ministry together. Perhaps this should have been identified first, since it seems foundational to everything else. It could have, yet worship also seemed foundational. So it is placed last— not least—for precisely the purpose of emphasis. In one sense, to speak about an overall focus on spirituality in a congregation's life seems to be stating the obvious, but in reality it is not. Congregations get caught up in keeping the institution going and hardly ever think about the centrality of staying connected to Jesus. In fact, it is nothing short of amazing how "unspiritual" churches can be in the sense that church membership as institutional involvement, apart from commitment to serious discipleship, is promoted. Except for the name "church" on the sign outside, a stranger would never know there was any difference between life in many churches and life in secular organizations. Prayer often becomes perfunctory, attendance and offerings become primary concerns, and "church work" serves as the barometer of "spiritual" health.

Everybody who goes to church knows this is the way church life has become for most congregations, which is one of the reasons there is such a hunger for something deeper. But leaders in the church are the key to changing the institutional focus of a congregation. It will not happen without intentionality. Every meeting should begin with a ten- to fifteen-minute worship experience. Decisions, as we have already mentioned, should be made within the context of the congregation's praying for discernment. Participation in small groups that seek to provide help for spiritual growth should be expected rather than recommended.

Raising the consciousness level of the need for the church's life to be rooted in the life of the Spirit seems a small thing. But it is one of those small things without which the church's life is not the same. More than that, a congregation whose members are not focused on spiritual growth and nurture in every aspect of their life together is a congregation in trouble, whether the members realize it or not. Institutional perpetuation is not synonymous with life in Christ. Once this is understood, spirituality will be the center of congregational life.

Some congregations are finding weekend retreats an effective way to raise the consciousness level of the entire church regarding spirituality, focusing on subjects ranging from the meaning of worship, the sharing of spiritual journey stories, or the life of a particular figure whose life is an inspiration, to learning the story of one's church and/or denomination. There also are two special types of prayer retreats people are finding to be a source of spiritual nurture and growth. One is the prayer retreat that allows people to step away from their routine for the sole purpose of being together in prayer, worship, and fellowship. Intentionality is the key. This is time devoted specifically to personal and collective prayer. It is not something tacked on to a meeting that has another agenda. Prayer retreats have one purpose—to take an extended period of time to learn about and experience praying in depth. Recreation and fellowship can be part of the schedule, but nothing should diminish the focus of the retreat on prayer.

A second type is the silent retreat. Led by someone experienced in this kind of retreat, the group spends the entire weekend in silence. Meals, free time, and community gatherings for worship are centered around silence. Participants discover in this extended time of silence a special opportunity to be attentive to the work of the Holy Spirit. Whenever I lead silent retreats, I tell participants to trust that if they listen, the Holy Spirit will bring them what they need in the silence. It does not matter what is going on in their personal lives. They can trust that the Spirit will bring them what they need. In twenty-five years of leading such retreats, I have never seen an instance where retreatants have not experienced the fruits of this trust.

One of the lessons people learn through silent retreats is that they communicate more intimately in silence than when they talk. Nonverbal communication is always stronger than verbal. People who live in community in silence learn to "speak" to one another through smiles and hugs, tears and withdrawals. It is amazing that people can be together an entire weekend or longer, never talking verbally, and conclude the time with a sense of being bonded in a way they did not know was possible. I have never known anyone who has not come away from a silent retreat without a deeper awareness of the presence of Jesus Christ than he or she had before. It is a special experience every church should offer its people.

The point of these kinds of retreats is to encourage and nurture a congregation in the one thing that is primary to its life—spiritual growth. This kind of growth has for too long been left up to individuals, without the collective life of the church offering any significant help. Christian spirituality is not just an individual experience. It is what the body of Christ as a whole ought to be living. Congregations serious about spirituality are well served to make a conscious effort to hold up its importance in every facet of their life together.

+ + +

Taking spirituality seriously in the church in the ways we have discussed may be the great challenge before us today. The church is a called community. This calling gives expression to the fact that as Christians we belong to Jesus first. Our relationship to one another begins in our relationship to him. The closer we grow to Jesus, the closer we grow to one another. The diagram of the wagon wheel that follows illustrates this point.

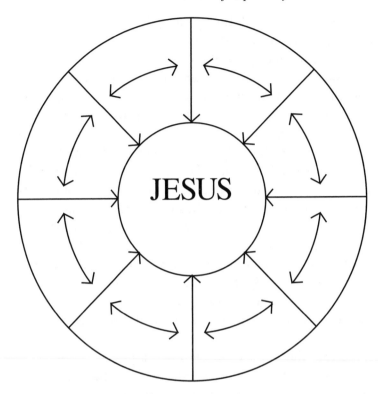

The diagram also underscores that which makes for a Christian community. It is the centrality of Jesus Christ. Nothing else makes community possible for Christians. What we are talking about is the heart of Christian mystery, stemming from the claim that Jesus was raised and is alive today. He draws us together. We do not possess the power to make ourselves into a community. As a community who claim the name of Jesus, we celebrate and witness to his presence. We commune with one another as we commune with him. This is what the Lord's Supper is all about. In the act of breaking bread, he makes himself known to those gathered, even as he did to the two on the Emmaus Road (Luke 24:13–35).

Part of the power of Christian spirituality is that it draws us into genuine community. The personal relationship Jesus' resurrection makes possible is never private. Loving him is always within the context of community with others who also know and love him. In Jesus we are made for each other, which is why loving him includes loving the way he loved. Genuine Christian spirituality is by nature communal. This is why the marvelous metaphor of the body the apostle Paul used for the church speaks a deep truth about life together in Jesus Christ.

The human body truly is, in the words of the psalmist, "fearfully and wonderfully made" (Psalm 139:14). It is the most marvelous and amazing system of relationships imaginable. Paul is suggesting that the wonder of the human body describes the church. The body of Christ is fearfully and wonderfully made. The incredible diversity within unity of the human body is true for the church. Each part has it own identity and function, but every part works for the health of the whole body. What better way to understand the church? The diversity each member brings to the body is celebrated within the context of the unity of the whole. Diversity without unity destroys the body. Unity without diversity destroys the spirit. Both are held together in the body's connectedness to the head. The brain gives direction to the individual parts and holds them together in unity. So it is with Jesus Christ. He is the church's unity.

What Paul did not say, but which is also true about the human body and the church, is that the wonder and gift of each are often taken for granted. Most of us have experienced the hard lesson of taking our bodies for granted. Churches make the same mistake. But in both instances we tend to keep doing the same thing. Here is where a disciplined spiritual life will serve us well personally and collectively as the church. The life of the Spirit is where we confront our neglect and find inspiration and power to change our ways. Attention to our spiritual needs helps us to step back and see what is happening to us and what can be done about it. We are such gifts. We can give so much to one another. But without focus on spiritual growth and nurture, we neglect the gifts we are.

The novel *Watership Down* by Richard Adams is a story about rabbits, and about human beings. At one point the traveling band around whom the story revolves has an experience that almost destroys them. Once they get to safety they realize that their failure to trust one another was the real danger they faced. Through the experience they learn something essential for their life together.

They had come closer together, relying on and valuing each other's capacities. They knew now that it was on these and on nothing else that their lives depended, and they were not going to waste anything they possessed between them. (Adams, 129)

Is this not a lesson in spiritual maturity for the church—never wasting anything we possess between us? Relying on and valuing each others' gifts and capacities is possible in congregations only as members realize their collective life must receive nourishment through a vital connectedness to Jesus, through a first-loyalty love for him and for loving the way he loved. This is the best spirituality any person and any church can practice. Nothing less is sufficient. Nothing more is required.

SELECTED
BIBLIOGRAPHY

*Titles listed below that were not cited in the text
are included as recommended reading.*

Adams, Richard. 1976. *Watership Down* (New York: Avon Books).

Baillie, John. 1962. *Christian Devotion* (New York: Scribners).

Baird-Middleton, Bruce. 1988. "Robert Coles: An Intimate Biographical Interview" (Cambridge: The Film Center, Harvard University).

Bell, Martin. 1968. *The Way of the Wolf* (New York: Seabury Press).

Bellah, Robert, et al. 1985. *Habits of The Heart* (New York: Harper & Row).

Bernard of Clairvaux. 1993. *The Love of God*, trans. by James Walton (Kalamazoo: Cistercian Publications).

Bloom, Anthony. 1945. *Beginning To Pray* (New York: Paulist Press).

Bonhoeffer, Dietrich. 1954. *Life Together* (New York: Harper & Row).

Buechner, Frederick. 1991. *Telling Secrets* (San Franscisco: HarperCollins).

Covey, Stephen. 1989. *The Seven Habits of Highly Effective People* (New York: Fireside).

De Mello, Anthony. 1991. *Contact With God* (Chicago: Loyola University Press).

Delp, Father. 1983. *The Prison Meditations of Father Delp* (New York: MacMillan).

Durback, Robert. 1990. *Seeds of Hope: A Henri Nouwen Reader* (New York: Bantam Books).

Eckhart, Meister. 1940. *Meister Eckhart*, trans. Raymond Blakney (New York: Harper & Bros.).

Edelman, Marian Wright. 1995. *Guide My Feet* (New York: Beacon Press) .

Edwards, Tilden. 1980. *Spiritual Friends* (New York: Paulist Press).

Eller, Vernard. 1973. *The Simple Life* (Grand Rapids: Eerdmans).

Emerson, Ralph Waldo. 1978. *Essays* (Westvaco).

Foster, Richard. 1978. *Celebration of Discipline* (San Francisco: Harper & Row).

Ignatius. 1983. *The Spiritual Exercises of St. Ignatius* (St. Louis: Image Books).

Jones, W. Paul. 1992. *Trumpet at Full Moon* (Louisville: Westminster/John Knox).

Julian of Norwich. 1988. *Reflections on Selected Texts* (Mystic, Conn.: Twenty-third Publications).

Kavanaugh, Kieran, ed. 1987. *St John of the Cross, Selected Writings: Classics in Western Spirituality* (New York: Paulist Press).

Keating, Thomas. 1986. *Open Mind, Open Heart* (Rockport: Element).

———. 1992. *Awakenings* (New York: Crossroad).

Kelley, Thomas. 1941. *Testament of Devotion* (New York: Harper & Row).

Kidd, Sue Monk. 1992. *When The Heart Waits* (San Franscisco: HarperCollins).

Kingsolver, Barbara. 1995. *High Tide in Tucson* (New York: HarperCollins).

Kinnamon, Katherine and Michael. 1990. *Everyday We Will Bless You* (St. Louis: CBP Press).

Law, William. 1978. *A Serious Call to the Devout and Holy Life* (New York: Paulist Press).

Lawrence, Brother. 1984. *Practicing The Presence of God* (Orleans, Mass.: Paraclete Press).

Linn, Jan G. 1994. *Living Inside Out* (St. Louis: Chalice Press).

May, Gerald. 1988. *Addiction and Grace* (San Franscisco: HarperCollins).

———. 1991. *The Awakened Heart* (San Franscisco: HarperCollins).

Mead, Loren. 1993. *The Once and Future Church* (Washington, D.C.: Alban Institute).

———. 1994. *Transforming Congregations for the Future* (Washington, D.C.: Alban Institute).

Merton, Thomas. 1961. *New Seeds of Contemplation* (New York: New Directions).

———. 1971. *Contemplative Prayer* (New York: Doubleday).

McCann, Dom Justin, ed. 1981. *The Cloud of Unknowing* (New York: Paulist Press).

Mulholland, Robert M., Jr. 1993. *Invitation To A Journey* (Downers Grove, Ill.: InterVarsity Press).

Niebuhr, Reinhold. 1932. *Moral Man and Immoral Society* (New York: Charles Scribner & Son).

Nouwen, Henri. 1972. *With Open Hands* (Notre Dame: Ave Maria Press).

———. 1974. *Out of Solitude* (Notre Dame: Ave Maria Press).

———. 1975. *Reaching Out* (New York: Doubleday).

———. 1977. *The Living Reminder* (New York: Seabury Press).

———. 1982. *Compassion: A Reflection on the Christian Life* (New York: Image Books).

———. 1983. *Gracias: A Latin American Journal* (San Franscisco: Harper & Row).

———. 1989. *In The Name of Jesus* (New York: Crossroad).

———. 1990. *The Road To Daybreak* (New York: Image Books).

———. 1993. *Life of The Beloved* (New York: Crossroad).

———. 1994. *Here and Now* (New York: Crossroad).

O'Connor, Elizabeth. 1963. *Call To Commitment* (New York: Harper & Row).

———. 1968 *Jouney Inward, Jouney Outward* (New York: Harper & Row).

Palmer, Parker. 1992. *The Active Life* (New York: HarperCollins).

Pascal, Blaise. 1958. *Pensees* (New York: E.P. Dutton & Co.).

Paulsell, William. 1990. *Tough Minds, Tender Hearts* (New York: Paulist Press).

———. 1992. *Taste and See*, rev. ed. (St. Louis: Chalice Press).

———. 1993. *Rules For Prayer* (New York: Paulist Press).

Pearson, Mark. 1990. *Christian Healing* (Grand Rapids: Chosen Books).

Peck, M. Scott. 1977. *The Road Less Traveled* (New York: Simon and Schuster).

Prevallet, Elaine. 1982. *Reflections On Simplicity* (Wallingford, Pa.: Pendle Hill, Pamphlet No. 244).

Reed, David A. 1990. *The Spiritual Health of the Episcopal Church* (New York: Episcopal Parish Services).

Runcorn, David. 1990. *A Center of Quiet* (Downers Grove, Ill.: InterVarsity Press).

Teresa, Mother. 1995. *A Simple Path* (New York: Ballantine Books).

Teresa of Avila. 1972. *Interior Castle*, ed. by E. Allison Peers (New York: Doubleday).

———. 1979. *The Interior Castle, Classics in Western Spirituality*, trans. by Kieran Kavanaugh and Otilio Rodrigues (New York: Paulist Press).

Thompson, Marjorie. 1995. *Soul Feast* (Louisville: Westminster/John Knox).

Tocqueville, Alexis de. 1899. *Democracy In America*, trans. by Henry Reeve (New York: The Colonial Press).

Vanier, Jean. 1989. *Community and Growth* rev. ed. (New York: Paulist Press).

Wells, Ron. 1982. *Spiritual Disciplines For Everyday Living* (Self-published).

Willard, Dallas. 1988. *The Spirit of The Disciplines* (San Francisco: HarperCollins).

Wuthnow, Robert. 1993. *Christianity in the 21st Century* (New York: Oxford University Press).

Zimmer, Mary. 1993. *Sister Images* (Nashville: Abingdon).